**FOREIGN POLICY ASSOCIATION**

## Headline Series

# ISLAM

## Politics and Religion in the Muslim World

by
**Thomas W. Lippman**

Foreword by
Malcolm C. Peck

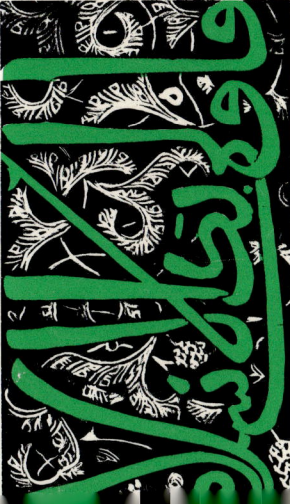

## A VALUABLE RESOURCE FOR TEACHERS AND STUDENTS

and a way to keep up to date on key foreign policy topics in the news . . .
Subscribe to the **HEADLINE Series**, published five times a year.

Each issue • is about a major world area or topic
- is written by a noted scholar
- is brief (usually 70 pages)
- is highly readable
- includes basic background, maps, charts, discussion guides and suggested reading

---

### Titles of Past Issues on Topics of Current Interest

| # | Title | Author | Year |
|---|---|---|---|
| 257 | Nigeria: Power and Democracy in Africa | by Jean Herskovits | 1982 |
| 256 | Polish Paradox: Communism and National Renewal | by William E. Schaufele, Jr. | 1981 |
| 255 | China's Four Modernizations and the U.S. | by Lynn Diane Feintech | 1981 |
| 254 | The ABC's of Defense: America's Military in the 1980s | by Christopher A. Kojm and the Editors of FPA | 1981 |
| 253 | The Caribbean: Its Implications for the United States | by Virginia R. Domínguez and Jorge I. Domínguez | 1981 |
| 252 | World Hunger: A Challenge to American Policy | by Sol M. Linowitz | 1980 |
| 251 | World Population: The Present and Future Crisis | by Phyllis T. Piotrow | 1980 |

---

### HOW TO ORDER

**Price per copy: $3.00**

Quantity Discounts

10-99 . . . . . 25% off     500-999 . . . . . 35% off
100-499 . . . . . 30% off    1000 or more . . . . . 40% off

Subscriptions

One year - $12.00
Two years - $20.00
Three years - $28.00

For information on all currently available **HEADLINE Series** and other FPA publications, write or call for a **free** catalog:

**Foreign Policy Association, 205 Lexington Avenue, New York, NY 10016**
**Deloris Gruber: (212) 481-8454**

FOREIGN POLICY ASSOCIATION
# Headline Series

No. 258   MARCH/APRIL 1982   $3.00

# ISLAM
## Politics and Religion in the Muslim World
by Thomas W. Lippman

*Foreword* by Malcolm C. Peck ...................... 3

**1** The Tide of Islam..................................... 7

**2** Islam in History ....................................... 18

**3** The Key Countries .................................. 34

| | |
|---|---|
| *Iran* | 34 |
| *Egypt* | 36 |
| *Turkey* | 41 |
| *Tunisia* | 43 |
| *Pakistan* | 45 |
| *Afghanistan* | 46 |
| *Saudi Arabia* | 48 |

**4** Lessons for Policy-makers........................ 54

*Talking It Over* .............................................. 63

Cover Design: Hersch Wartik

University of Charleston Library
Charleston, WV  25304
105276

297.1977
L667i
1982

# The Author

THOMAS W. LIPPMAN, reporter, editor and foreign correspondent of *The Washington Post,* developed his interest in Islam when he was a visiting professor at American University in Cairo and in the four years he covered the Middle East for the *Post.* Upon his return in 1979, he continued his research on the Middle East as Edward R. Murrow Fellow at the Council on Foreign Relations. Born in New York, he is a graduate of Columbia University. His book, *Understanding Islam: An Introduction to the Moslem World,* was recently published by New American Library.

*Photo by Frank Johnston,* The Washington Post

# The Foreign Policy Association

The Foreign Policy Association is a private, nonprofit, nonpartisan educational organization. Its purpose is to stimulate wider interest and more effective participation in, and greater understanding of, world affairs among American citizens. Among its activities is the continuous publication, dating from 1935, of the HEADLINE SERIES pamphlets. The authors of these pamphlets are responsible for factual accuracy and for the views expressed. FPA itself takes no position on issues of United States foreign policy.

---

The HEADLINE SERIES (ISSN 0017-8780) is published January, March, May, September and November by the Foreign Policy Association, Inc., 205 Lexington Ave., New York, N.Y. 10016. President, William E. Schaufele, Jr.; Editor, Nancy L. Hoepli; Associate Editor, Ann R. Monjo; Assistant Editor, Mary E. Stavrou. Subscription rates, $12.00 for 5 issues; $20.00 for 10 issues; $28.00 for 15 issues. Single copy price $3.00. Discount 25% on 10 to 99 copies; 30% on 100 to 499; 35% on 500 to 999; 40% on 1,000 or more. Payment must accompany order for $5 or less. Second-class postage paid at New York, N.Y. Copyright 1982 by Foreign Policy Association, Inc. Composed and printed at Science Press, Ephrata, Pa.

Library of Congress Catalog No. 82-71037
ISBN 0-87124-075-0

# Foreword
by Malcolm C. Peck

The introduction to Islam for many Americans was the trauma of the hostage crisis and the shock of bitter Iranian denunciations of the United States as the "great Satan." The Islamic revolution in Iran brought dramatically and painfully to Americans' attention the power of Islam as a motivating force in contemporary affairs. It also indicated the urgent need to learn something of the basic attitudes and concerns of some 800 million Muslims around the world.

The generally negative and hostile face of Islam which the events in Teheran presented on American television reinforced an unfortunate historical legacy. Centuries of Christian-Muslim hot and cold war (which did not exclude periods of fruitful cultural exchange) created hostile perceptions of Islam in the West. Later, Western colonial rule over most Muslim populations, and the literature justifying it, tended to foster an image of Islam as backward and exotic. In the virtual absence of accurate, informed works on Islam, negative and distorted notions have colored Western attitudes and presented a serious obstacle to understanding. We can no longer afford this intellectual failing.

While Ayatollah Khomeini's Islamic revolution in Iran does not provide an accurate expression of the views of most Muslims,

*This is one of a number of issues of the HEADLINE SERIES, dealing with international topics of special humanistic significance, whose publication in the period 1980–83 is being supported by the National Endowment for the Humanities.*

it does reflect a profound concern throughout the Muslim world community over erosion of the central moral values which have preserved it through 14 centuries. The revolution and its reverberations elsewhere are in large measure a reaction against what is perceived as the moral bankruptcy of imported alien values. This not only involves behavior which is obviously contrary to established Islamic norms but touches upon the essence of the distinction between objectivization of the world and acknowledgment of God's primacy as the single source of all existence. Whatever causes people to cease to acknowledge that unqualified primacy, which is the central truth of Islam, is evil. It is this which lies behind Khomeini's accusations of "Satanism" against America. It is this also which strikes a resonant chord with many Muslims, leading them to see the need to restructure a proper Islamic way of life for the individual and society, though most of them would shun—even abhor—Khomeini's excesses.

What also makes social and political actions in Iran and other Muslim countries specifically Islamic is the relationship between religion and politics. Separation of church and state is a concept alien to Islam. Though in practice there has been a degree of separation since early Islamic history, religion and politics remain intimately connected today. As one observes events in Iran it is often impossible to say whether religion masks political motives or the reverse. Moreover, secular ideologies have not really taken root in most Muslim countries, so that Islam strongly influences the political process and shapes the actions of even secular-minded leaders.

Nevertheless, the Iranian model will not, contrary to some suggestions, be successfully exported. While there is a very real sense of Muslim solidarity, there is slight prospect of common political action on important issues. Within the very real unity of belief and emotion, which has helped to promote a widespread upsurge of religious expression, there exists a rich diversity of cultural and historical experience across the world of Islam.

If there are "crescents of crisis" endangering American interests, they are not of Islamic origin. The United States will always have varying political relations with Muslim countries, and it is both practically self-defeating as well as morally objectionable to identify "good" and "bad" Muslims as they may serve or oppose American purposes. Rather it is necessary to understand Islam and its adherents on their own terms.

Thus seen, Islam reveals a considerable capacity for pragmatic and flexible adaptation to changing circumstances. In the light of much recent loose discussion of the danger of instability in Saudi Arabia's conservative Muslim society, it is instructive to inquire how many other societies could absorb the massive changes visited upon that one in the same unprecedentedly brief span of time and still remain intact. Conservative Muslims believe that it is possible indefinitely to insulate Islamic society from the cultural and intellectual baggage which Western technology brings in its train. It may be left to scholarly speculation whether in fact this can continue into the future and whether Islam can periodically revitalize itself through reform from within, as it is now doing, or whether, eventually, it must pass through something like the Reformation which reshaped Western Christianity.

Whatever the future may hold, Islam today is a vital force among one fifth of the world's population. It is important for Americans to understand better a faith and culture until now little known in the West. This should be not merely an exercise for policy-makers absorbed with strategic, political and economic interests in the Muslim world but an urgent assignment for all thoughtful Americans with a human concern for those many people around the world who are part of a great religious-cultural tradition related closely to our own.

Thomas Lippman's study is thus especially welcome in providing an introduction to Islam in its historical and contemporary settings. This is particularly the case because the subject is usually left to narrowly focused scholars, apologists or polemicists. Mr. Lippman's work is balanced and insightful and deserves to be read widely and attentively.

---

Dr. Peck, director of programs of The Middle East Institute, is president of the board of Islam Centennial Fourteen, a national nonprofit organization providing educational and cultural events in honor of the 14 centuries of Islam. On leave from the institute, he is currently Arabian Peninsula Affairs analyst with the Department of State.

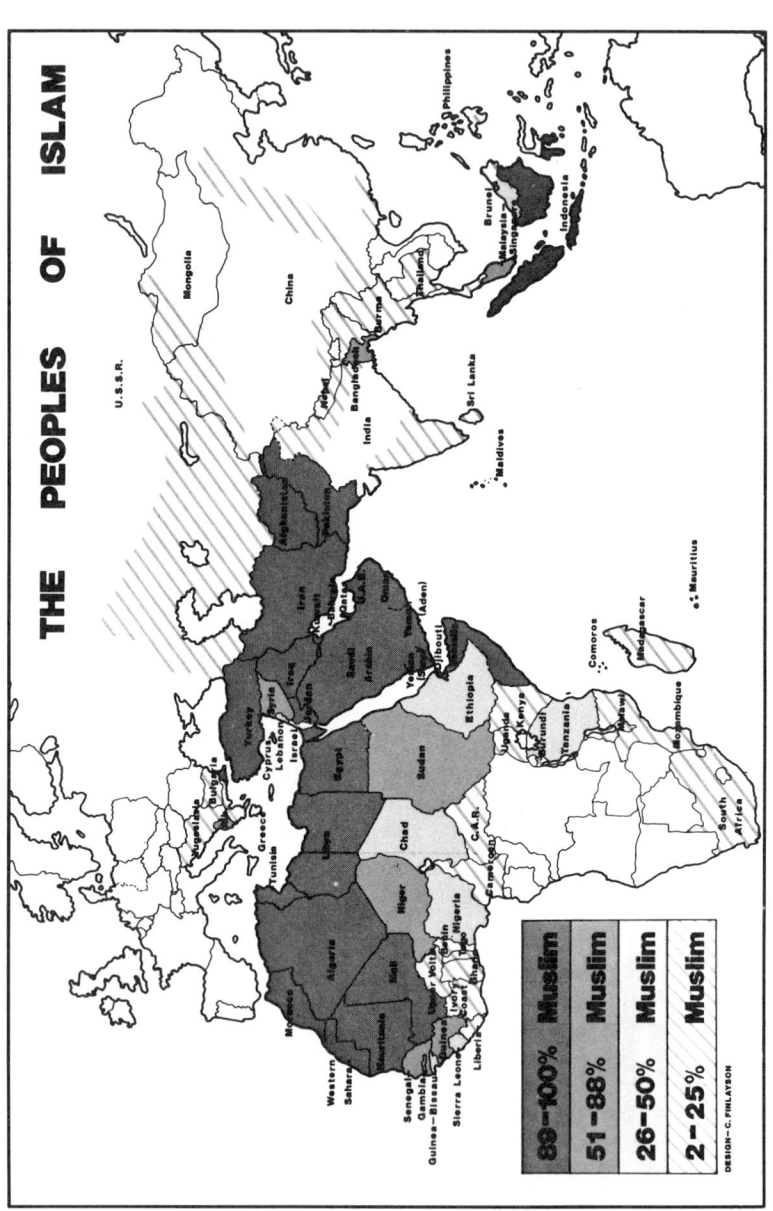

# 1

# The Tide of Islam

The assassination of President Anwar el-Sadat of Egypt on October 6, 1981, and the uprising by religious extremists in the Nile river city of Asyut that followed it, focused Western attention once again on what appears to be a rising tide of fundamentalism, xenophobia and violence in the Muslim world.

On the surface, it appeared that the same religious fervor that swept away the shah of Iran and challenged the regimes of Syria, Tunisia and other states had struck Egypt. The world of Islam, where the volatile mix of religion and politics seems to lead to chronic instability, was subjected to anxious scrutiny in Washington, Tokyo and European capitals, where oil supplies might have to be protected and defense arrangements might be jeopardized.

The shock of Sadat's death was more profound in Washington than it was in Cairo; the Egyptian people seemed largely indifferent to the passing of a leader who had not fulfilled their hopes, but the Americans depended on him. The United States had only recently recovered from the loss of a key ally in Iran and the ordeal of the hostages, and its entire strategic policy in the Middle East and South Asia rested on three other Muslim nations: Egypt, Saudi Arabia and Pakistan. If, as Sadat's death made it appear, Muslim states are inherently unstable, or if Islam is incompatible with pro-Western strategy in international affairs, then the entire U.S. policy—including the sale to Saudi Arabia of sophisticated AWACS radar surveillance planes, which President Ronald Reagan was then trying to push through Congress—was open to question.

## *Religion and State*

The irony of Sadat's assassination was that he had warned for many years against mingling religion and politics in public life. He knew perfectly well, he often said, that in Islam religion and the state are one, but he sought to separate them in affairs of government.

In *Revolt on the Nile*, a memoir of the 1952 revolution that he wrote a quarter-century before his death, Sadat said he had learned that "religion is one thing, its exploitation for political purposes quite another. It must not be given a purpose which it does not inherently possess. If a religion is turned into a political system, then fanaticism is born. This confusion of temporal power with the spiritual has been the downfall of many Oriental societies."

As president, Sadat had banned political parties based on religion, and he repeatedly warned university students not to impose their religious convictions on others. He tolerated the activities of conservative religious groups, which he regarded as a useful counterforce to the leftist elements he most feared, but a month before his death he ordered a mass roundup of religious extremists, together with other critics and opponents of his government. Because of his personal fame as the Arab leader who made peace with Israel and his critical position in Washington's strategic calculations, his moves were widely publicized; but Sadat was hardly alone among Islamic political leaders in his struggle to balance religious sentiment with public policy. Tunisia, Turkey, Indonesia, Sudan, Nigeria, Pakistan, Malaysia, Saudi Arabia and, of course, Iran face similar issues.

Early in 1979, Hafizullah Amin, the foreign minister in Afghanistan's leftist revolutionary government, issued a blunt warning to the country's religious hierarchy. "Those religious leaders who are busy with religious performances and do not act against the interest of the people and the revolution will be respected profoundly by us," he said. "But those who instead of serving the sacred religion of Islam use religion as a means to serve the enemies of the revolution will face repercussions."

At about the same time, Shahpur Bakhtiar, the last prime minister installed by the shah, expressed a similar view of the proper role for Iran's religious establishment. "The eminent ayatollahs' position," he told parliament, "is far above entering into the political arena in the way you and I are engaged in here. They should guide and direct us in their spiritual capacity and tell us that the government should in this or that issue be inspired by the lofty teachings of Islam." In other words, this French-educated politician, like his American-educated counterpart in Afghanistan, did not believe that the country should be run by its religious leaders.

Amin, Bakhtiar and Sadat were totally dissimilar politicians in different circumstances, but the problem they faced is common to all rulers of Muslim countries. Religion and politics cannot be entirely separated, and the ruling authority in a Muslim country cannot insulate itself from judgment by religious standards.

That is because Islam is by its nature an activist faith that in principle accepts no distinction between church and state or between lay and religious affairs. The Christian doctrine of separation between that which is Caesar's and that which is God's is alien to Islam, and Muslims are untrue to the precepts of their faith if they refrain from religious involvement in matters of state.

Muhammad of Mecca, the Arabian prophet of the seventh century A.D. who established the Islamic religion, laid down to his followers the principle that morality requires involvement. "Whosoever of you sees an evil action, let him change it with his hand," he said, "and if he is not able to do so, then with his tongue; and if he is not able to do so, then with his heart—and that is the weakest of faith."

In Islam, to believe is to act. Islam is an Arabic word meaning submission—submission to the will of God. A Muslim (the word is the participial form of Islam) is one who submits to God. But submission does not mean passivity. Submission to God's will may well require action in earthly affairs, to defend the faith or attack evil. No earthly or man-made law can be above the moral code laid down in the Koran (or Quran), the Muslim holy book that records God's revelations to Muhammad.

Muhammad envisioned the creation of an Islamic state, a community of Muslims run by Muslims according to the rules of the faith. As prophet, judge, lawgiver, military commander and social arbiter of his followers, he was the head of such a community while he lived; but he did not specify how the Muslim community was to be governed after his death or how Islam could adapt itself to a heterogeneous society. Muslims today can argue with equal sincerity that Islam requires a republican government or that Islam is best embodied in a monarchy.

### *Diversity of Islam*

There is no single Islamic world view, no one Muslim way of looking at life, government and statecraft. Libya's Muammar al-Qaddafi claims to be running an Islamic state, but Saudi Arabian religious leaders have accused him of heresy. Iran's Ayatollah Ruhollah Khomeini maintains he is the arbiter of Islamic values, but Sadat denounced him as an apostle of hatred who betrayed the spirit of Islamic justice and mercy. Iran and Iraq are Muslim countries, but they have been at war since 1980—and the Kurds, who are also Muslims, rise up periodically against both Iran and Iraq because they seek a state of their own based on ethnic, not religious, foundations.

Islam professes to regulate all aspects of life; but it offers only guidelines and principles for the governance of the community of believers, not a constitution. A body of Islamic law, the *shari'ah*, has been developed to apply the principles of the Koran to specific problems and cases, but it cannot cover every legal contingency in today's world and in any case is being reinterpreted to meet changing needs. It is only natural, therefore, that in any Muslim society, reformers, revolutionaries, dissenters and opportunists should appear from time to time, and that, whatever their political views, they should claim to be acting in the name of Islam.

In the words of Metin Heper, a Turkish social scientist, religion offers a "functional alternative to politics" in countries where political activity of a more conventional type, through parties, trade unions and parliaments, is restricted. Political parties and student groups may be suppressed, but incendiary ideas or pleas for reform issued in the name of the Koran and the prophet cannot be so easily dismissed.

Furthermore, Islam provides a useful coloration for any gang of terrorists or usurpers who seek power. Any group can style itself Islamic; whether it actually represents the principles of the faith is another matter. Islam promises the rewards of Paradise to those who fight against evil, but that does not mean that Islam stands for executions, assassinations, café-bombings or even the imposition of Koranic law on contemporary societies.

Because Islam encompasses all aspects of life, it is natural and inevitable that in times of stress, upheaval or social change the banners of the faith should be raised over political movements; the faith has stirred the believers to action for 14 centuries, and by the same token those who wish to act, whatever their true motives, have acted in the name of the faith. Islam in the contemporary world represents moral strength and cultural continuity, national pride and personal dignity. To Muslims seeking to rid themselves of the vestiges of imperial domination, shelter themselves against the intrusion of alien cultures and find meaning in lives of poverty and deprivation, closer adherence to Islamic teachings and traditions offers the answer.

## *One Code, Many Applications*

All Muslims share one heritage and subscribe to one collective code of justice and morality, but the political situation in each Muslim country—the way that code of justice is applied—must be analyzed separately. The way in which Islamic consciousness is expressed varies from country to country, community to community. There is no single worldwide "Islamic resurgence," but there has been a series of coincident upheavals in which Islam is the common expression of political dissent.

Student activism in Egypt and Afghan resistance to the Soviet invasion of 1979 are not related to each other, or to the Iranian revolution: the Afghan guerrillas and the Egyptian students may admire the Iranian revolution and wish to emulate it, but they are not acting because of it. They are acting because of developments in their own countries and to defend their own culture and traditions against the perceived encroachments of immoral or alien influences. Sectarian strife in Lebanon, religious agitation in Tunisia, and the rise to power of military dictators posing as religious leaders in Libya and Pakistan are the results of history and conditions in the nations where they occur, not manifestations of a coordinated international movement.

Fundamentalism, in the sense of close adherence to Koranic precepts, has a growing transnational appeal. The triumph of fundamentalist views in a given country, however, need not necessarily be inimical to U.S. interests, as the case of Saudi Arabia shows. Each religious movement has to be examined in its own context. To have constructive relationships with devout Muslims, it is necessary to view their history and culture with respect instead of alarm and to conduct dealings with an appreciation of local conditions and sensitivities.

Centuries of war, poverty, and colonial domination sapped the political strength of the Islamic peoples. One by one the great Islamic empires of the Arabs, the Persians, the Moghuls in India, and the Ottomans wore themselves out and crumbled before hostile forces. As the conquerors came and went, religion remained the source of cultural continuity for the Muslim people, their fount of history, education, philosophy and law. Now the Muslims have largely regained their independence of foreign domination and are again assertive. Electronic communications and jet travel have enhanced their cultural ties to each other—the annual pilgrimage to Mecca attracts a million or more each year and its rites are televised throughout the Muslim world—and have helped Muslims regain their collective pride and sense of community.

It is no longer necessary for a Muslim to mimic the British or the French or the Italians to advance himself in the world. If his vision of the future excludes coeducation, alcohol, political parties, parliamentary government or the English language, it may appear hostile and threatening to Americans and Europeans, but it is entirely justifiable in its own context.

The choices made by one country or society, however, do not necessarily affect those of another. In international affairs, Islam is frequently irrelevant: Saudi Arabia's oil-pricing policies, for example, and Algeria's desire to prevent Morocco from annexing the Western Sahara have nothing to do with religion.

Between the end of World War II and the tragic Lebanese civil war that began in 1975, the most important inter-Arab political conflict was that between Iraq and Egypt over Iraq's participation in the Baghdad Pact of 1955. The Baghdad Pact was an American-sponsored anti-Communist defense alliance that linked Britain with Iraq, Turkey, Pakistan and Iran—four Muslim countries. The participation of so many Muslims did not placate Egypt's President Gamal Abdel Nasser; he saw the pact as a masterstroke of imperialism and set out to undo it. The resulting struggle split the Arab world into pro-Western and pro-Soviet camps, touched off years of turmoil in Egypt, Iraq, Jordan and Lebanon, was one factor in provoking Nasser into nationalizing the Suez Canal—thus igniting the Suez war of 1956—and eventually led to the bloody overthrow of the Hashemite monarchy in Iraq. The echoes are still being heard in the Middle East. But Islam, as a religion, played no part in the struggle. The principal actors, Nasser of Egypt, Nuri as-Said of Iraq, Adnan Menderes of Turkey, King Husayn of Jordan, were all Muslims, but their decisions were based on such pragmatic considerations as Soviet and American intentions, arms supplies, regional influence and oil markets, not on religion.

The same is true of most international political decisions made by Muslim states. They do not generally allow religion to intrude upon practical considerations. The only other valid generalization about the Islamic world is that it defies generalization. Dar al-Islam, the House of Islam, embraces as many as 800 million people, of every race, from Senegal to China and from Nigeria to the Soviet Union. The adherents of the faith naturally differ as widely in social and economic behavior as they do in history; they cannot be stereotyped. Certainly the cartoonists' equation of Muslims with polygamous Arabs flaunting their oil wealth cannot be justified: the vast majority of Muslims are not Arabs, not wealthy, and not polygamous.

The three biggest Muslim nations are Indonesia, with about 135 million Muslims (about equal to the population of all the Arab states together); Pakistan, with 80 million; and Bangladesh, with 75 million. The largest Arab nation, Egypt, has about 40 million Muslims in a population that also includes several million Christians. The list of countries where the population is more than half Muslim includes Mali, Afghanistan, Malaysia, and of course Iran and Turkey—none of which is an Arab state.

All the figures in that vast tapestry share certain moral, legal and eschatological beliefs. They believe in one God, who is essentially the same as the Hebrew God of the Old Testament, and they believe that God's word was revealed to mankind through a series of prophets whose revelations are recorded in holy scriptures. The last of the prophets was Muhammad; the final holy book, the one that explained and rectified all others, is the Koran.

The line of prophets includes Abraham, Moses, Noah and Jesus. All the prophets, including Jesus and Muhammad, were mortal men, without divine attributes; the uniqueness and oneness of God is the central doctrine of Islam. The Islamic religion specifically repudiates the Christian doctrine of the trinity, which in the Muslim view is tantamount to polytheism.

### *Five Pillars of Faith*

All Muslims, in principle, accept the shari'ah, the code of laws that regulates behavior, social relationships, property and commerce. And virtually all Muslims agree that the ideals and duties of the faith are embodied in the so-called Five Pillars: 1. the profession of faith, the declaration that there is no god but God and Muhammad is the messenger of God; 2. ritual prayer five

The late Egyptian President Anwar el-Sadat (second from left) was a devout Muslim. Although he knew well that in Islam religion and the state are one, he sought to separate them in affairs of government.

times a day; 3. payment of the *zakat* or alms-tax, analogous to tithing; 4. fasting during Ramadan, one of the months of the Islamic lunar calendar; 5. the pilgrimage to Mecca, which all Muslims are obliged to make once if they are able.

Within that framework, there are vast differences in wealth, societal patterns, race, community structure and history—differences as great as those between, for example, Sweden and El Salvador among Christian countries. Monarchies and republics claim the sanction of Islam with equal fervor. Socialist states justify their policies as a fulfillment of the Koran's rules about social justice; free-enterprisers denounce socialism as a violation of Koranic rules governing private property. No rulers could be more different in personal style and system of governance than

**Major Islamic Cities at the Time of the Crusades**

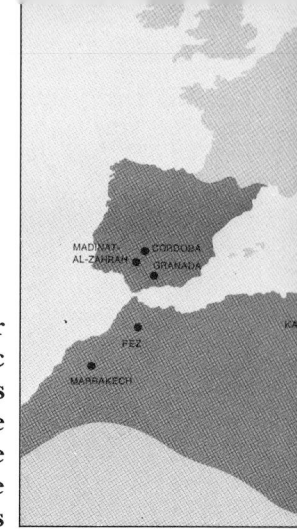

Egypt's Sadat and Iran's Khomeini. The two men loathed each other and regarded each other as corrupt and heretical, yet both ruled as Muslims in countries where Islam is the official religion.

All Muslims participate in a spiritual brotherhood exemplified by the pilgrimage, which brings together as equals before God Muslims of every political, racial and economic background. But political unity within Islam did not survive the death of the Caliph Umar, and there is no prospect of restoring it. Despite solemn declarations about unity of purpose and aspiration from international Islamic conferences, Muslims continue as they have for centuries to fight each other at least as often as they fight unbelievers.

In the richly diverse world community of Islam, it is a drastic oversimplification to talk of fundamentalism or extremism as a single phenomenon; one man's fundamentalism is another's fanaticism, and one country's extremism is another's standing policy. Saudi Arabia, for example, already has a system that would be regarded as extremist if proposed for Tunisia or Turkey: the Koran is the sole source of law, basic domestic policies are set by religious rules, and the state enforces traditional social patterns. Yet even Saudi Arabia has not escaped

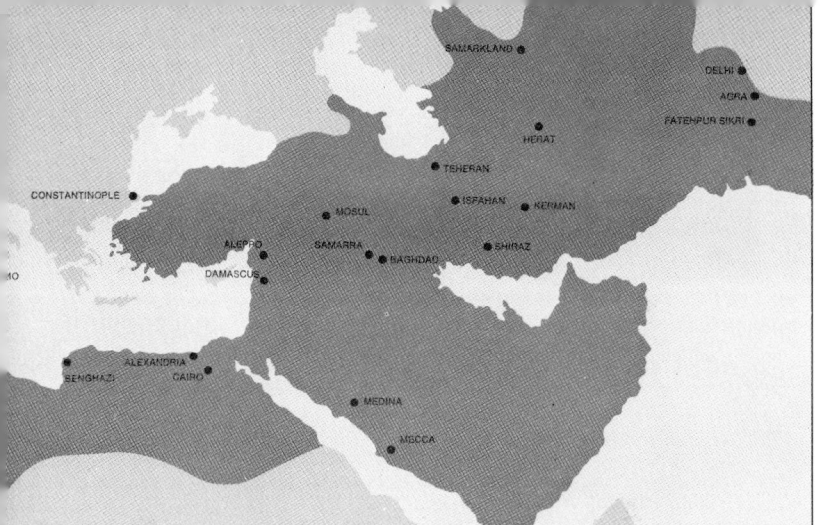

agitation by religiously motivated terrorists who find the atmosphere too permissive.

In general, however, the various groups and individuals who are described in the press as fundamentalists and whose recent activities are said to constitute a general resurgence of Islam do share certain principles and objectives. They want the shari'ah to be the basis of civil and criminal legal codes in their community; that usually means strict criminal laws, bans on alcohol, usury, gambling and pornography, separation of the sexes in school and workplace, and religious training in the schools. In a larger sense, they want full public support for a way of life based on their Islamic heritage, purged of materialism and amoral behavior they see as a consequence of the corrupting influence of the West.

Even in non-Arab countries, these movements often align themselves with Arab nationalist causes, especially that of the Palestinians. The first foreign policy initiative of the revolutionary government in Iran was to sever Iran's ties to Israel and establish relations with the Palestine Liberation Organization (PLO). In general, however, their immediate objectives are domestic, not international. Their goal is the primacy of the Islamic way of life; their problem is to define it in a way that satisfies the majority of the community.

# 2

# Islam in History

Islam has had a martial history since the beginning of the faith but since its first century it has been spread more by peaceful infiltration than by force of arms. The Battle of Tours, or Poitiers, in 732, exactly 100 years after the death of Muhammad, ended the advance of Islam into Western Europe. There have been few if any incidents since then in which Islamic states or rulers attacked non-Muslims solely for religious reasons. The advance of the Ottoman Turks into the Balkans, for example, was motivated as much by imperial as by religious objectives, and Christians within the conquered states retained a measure of autonomy.

Islam originated with Muhammad, who was born in Mecca, in what is now Saudi Arabia, in about 570. There was at the time no unified nation on the Arabian peninsula. Tribal hierarchies and clan loyalties formed the basis of the social structure. Pre-Islamic Arabia was by all accounts a violent society, characterized by vendetta, infanticide and banditry; in religion, the people were mostly pagan polytheists.

Monotheism was not unknown. Many Jews lived in Arabia, and the Arabians had frequent contact, through trade and war, with Christians in Syria and Ethiopia. But the prevalent religion was the worship of a variety of petty deities whose headquarters, so to speak, was a shrine at Mecca called the Kaabah. Muhammad's grandfather was custodian of the shrine, a position of some prominence because it was customary for Arabians to visit the Kaabah as pilgrims, and the pilgrimage traffic was a cornerstone of Mecca's commercial prosperity.

Muhammad's father died before he was born, his mother, when he was six. He was entrusted to the care of relatives. His uncle, Abu Talib, became his guardian and protector.

Little is known of Muhammad's youth. He had no formal education and apparently remained illiterate all his life. Muslim tradition holds that he was handsome, serious and virtuous, but there is no reliable record of any specific accomplishments until he was well into adulthood.

At 25 he married Khadijah, a wealthy widow many years older than he. She bore six children. Unhappily for Muhammad and for Islam, no son lived into manhood, and when the prophet died, a dispute over the succession to his temporal authority created a split in the faith that endures to this day. By all other measures, the marriage seems to have been a great success, and Muhammad took no other wife while Khadijah lived, though plural marriage was common. He married several other women after Khadijah died, including a Jew and a Christian.

### *The God of Islam*

It was Muhammad's custom to retire occasionally to a cave outside Mecca for meditation and there, on a night in the month now celebrated as Ramadan, when he was about 40 years old, his religious experiences began. Muslims believe that the angel Gabriel appeared and commanded, "Recite!" or "Proclaim!" Muhammad asked, "what shall I recite?" and the angel responded, as recorded in *Surah* (chapter) 96 of the Koran, "Recite in the name of your Lord who created, created man from clots of blood! Recite! Your Lord is the Most Bountiful One, who by the pen taught man what he did not know."

Muslims believe these revelations are the direct, literal word of

God, not written by Muhammad but dictated to him. They continued throughout the rest of Muhammad's life and were compiled after he died by others who had heard what he said. God commanded Muhammad to preach a new faith—or, more accurately, a rectification of existing monotheistic faith, which had been corrupted—based on absolute submission to the one true God, social justice, and a sense of religious community that would transcend tribal and regional affiliations.

*Allah* is the Arabic word for God, used by Muslims and Christians alike. The God of Islam is the God of the Old Testament, not a new deity invented by Muhammad, and Muslims believe that Muhammad was the last, rectifying prophet of a line traceable back to Abraham.

From the beginning, the message of Islam was that belief alone was not sufficient to gain entry into Paradise. The virtuous life requires action, social reform, and confrontation with evil wherever it is encountered. Prayer is required, but to fulfill God's commands it is also necessary to behave justly in society. For the Arabians of the seventh century, that meant it was required, as the Koran said, to trade honestly, treat women well, care for orphans, forgo usury and abandon infanticide. For contemporary Muslims, the evils are less clearly defined, so that while Muslims are encouraged by their faith to act, to move against evil, to seek social reform, there is no one program by which all Muslims can fulfill that duty. There is no central source of religious authority or doctrinal interpretation in Islam. It is a religion without a priesthood—no rite of ordination elevates any man into a special relationship with God—and therefore no equivalent of the Vatican. As a result, divergence of opinion on how the commands of the Koran should be applied today is almost guaranteed.

In Muhammad's lifetime, he was the sole arbiter of religious questions, as well as judge and military commander. At first he made few converts among the Meccans. In the three years after the first revelation, his revolutionary program is said to have attracted only 30 adherents, including Khadijah.

Making little headway with his preaching and harassed by the Quraish, Mecca's ruling tribe, Muhammad was obliged to leave the city of his birth. A delegation from a town called Yathrib—now known as Medina—invited him to establish himself there, and although the conversion of Mecca remained his goal, he was obliged to accept.

On September 24 in the year 622, Muhammad and his followers completed their migration to Medina, about 280 miles north of Mecca. That trek, called *hijra* in Arabic, or hegira, marked the beginning of the rise of Islam. The Muslim calendar dates from that year.

The Medinese had no vested interest in the commerce of the pilgrimage, which might suffer if a new creed were adopted, and they had no tribal hostility to Muhammad. Because their city had been divided by civil strife, they welcomed Muhammad as a stabilizing force, an arbitrator and decision-maker who could impose order on an unruly society. Almost overnight, the scorned prophet of Mecca was transformed into the respected leader of a community. He was not only its religious leader but a magistrate, lawgiver and military commander as well.

The remaining decade of Muhammad's life was marked by the development of Islam as a religion and as a social system—setting the rules for taxation, divorce, and inheritance, and establishing standards for commercial and criminal codes—and by repeated skirmishes with the Quraish as Muhammad sought to return to Mecca. He wanted to reclaim the Kaabah from the pagans and purge it of idols; he taught, and Muslims believe, that the shrine was first built by the patriarch Abraham and only later taken over by polytheists. Muhammad, living at Medina, abandoned Jerusalem in favor of Mecca as the geographic pole of ritual prayer for Muslims and incorporated the pilgrimage into Islam. Now it was necessary to gain control of Mecca itself.

The Quraish failed in a series of attacks on the Muslims at Medina, and then it was Muhammad's turn to make a move. In the first important military engagement, the "battle of Badr," in March 624, a Muslim force of 300 defeated nearly 1,000 Meccans, an outcome taken as a sign of God's endorsement of Muhammad's mission.

Alternating confrontation and negotiation, he extracted from the Quraish the right to return to Mecca as a pilgrim. Then in January 630 he marched on Mecca with an army of 10,000 men and met little resistance as the Quraish military commander came over to the side of the Muslims. Muhammad and his followers marched into Mecca and destroyed the wooden idols in the Kaabah. The triumph of Islam in Arabia thus assured, Muhammad returned to Medina, where he died in 632.

## *Islamic Empire*

The Koran was revealed in Arabic and the text stresses that Islam is an Arabian religion, bringing divine revelation to people who, unlike Jews and Christians, had no holy book. It is not clear whether Muhammad envisioned Islam as a universal faith that encompassed non-Arabians, but with his death the new leaders of the community wasted little time before undertaking armed campaigns that would soon carry Islam far beyond Arabia.

The lands of Asia Minor and the rim of the Mediterranean, exhausted by endless wars between the Byzantine and Persian empires, were easy prey for the disciplined armies that swept out of the Arabian peninsula. Within 100 years of the prophet's death, the Arabian Muslims were masters of a vast territory that extended from the south of France to the Indus river. Their empire included North Africa and Egypt, all of the Arabian peninsula, Palestine and the Fertile Crescent, Persia and much of central Asia and western India. Islam was transformed from a straightforward faith centered in one relatively unsophisticated culture into a complex and subtle theological and legal system incorporating Persian, Greek, Roman and Christian concepts and doctrines.

The wars that created the Arab empire represented the greatest triumphs of Arab arms and are part of every Muslim's historic consciousness; the great generals, such as Amr ibn-al-As, conqueror of Egypt, and Khalid ibn al-Walid, the "sword of Allah," who took Damascus, are still admired, and their feats are known to every schoolboy. In general, however, their campaigns of conquest were not wars of religious conversion. The great majority of people in the conquered lands embraced Islam, but not because they were forced to do so. Egypt, for example, welcomed the Muslim invaders, who appeared to the Egyptians not as oppressors but as liberators from the harsh rule of the Byzantines. More than 200 years elapsed before a majority of the population in Egypt abandoned Christianity for Islam.

It was a Muslim empire, ruled by Muslims, with the Arabian Muslims at the top of the power structure and new converts below them. Christians and Jews who retained their faith were accorded a special place as "people of the book," monotheists who practiced a religion revealed by God through scripture. They paid a special tax that exempted them from military service, and some historians say the Muslim rulers actually discouraged conversion to Islam because it reduced the state revenues. Muhammad expelled all the Jews from Medina because he believed they supported the Quraish against the Muslims and broke a pact he had made with them, and the Koran speaks harshly about them; but the prophet's temporal successors, the caliphs, used Jews and Christians as administrators and civil servants in most parts of the empire outside the Arabian peninsula.

The principle that paganism was to be abolished but Judaism and Christianity respected has remained part of Islamic doctrine ever since, though it has not always been followed. When Sadat, just before his death, cracked down on Muslim extremists who were harassing Christians, he gave them this message: "The Muslim president of the Muslim state does not accept that any harm should befall any of his citizens, particularly if these citizens are adherents of a revealed religion, that is to say, the Christians and the Muslims." He omitted the Jews, but the principle applies to them as well and Sadat had included them in earlier pronouncements. (In the mid-1970s, several Arab states, including Iraq and Morocco, acknowledged that they had erred in expelling Jewish citizens after the creation of Israel and invited them to return. Their motives were suspect—they probably wished to undercut Israel by taking people away from it—but their act was in accordance with the principles of Islam.)

The rapid military expansion of the Islamic empire led to an explosion of learning and mass cultural absorption that turned the Islamic world into the world's repository of science and philosophy; but the empire's political cohesion unraveled as rapidly as its intellectual and artistic achievements grew.

Muhammad designated no successor as ruler of the Islamic community, and he established no constitution and no system for lawmaking in new contexts. As a result, Muslim began to fight Muslim within 30 years after the prophet's death. His doctrine of the brotherhood of Islam, of a single community ruled by consensus according to the principles of the faith, was undermined by political rivalry and factional intrigue. Muslims still profess to adhere to the prophet's doctrine, but as a practical matter it was abandoned 1,200 years ago. However, it remains important as a symbolic ideal to which appeal is frequently made.

## *Sunnite vs. Shiite*

The most important division, which arose immediately after the prophet's death and endures to this day, originated in a disagreement over the succession to Muhammad's temporal authority. Muhammad was the last prophet and revelation ended with him; no one could inherit his religious role. But the existence of the Islamic community required someone to run it—a ruler who would conduct the affairs of the community according to the principles of Islam and defend the faith against infidels. In the absence of a divinely sanctioned formula for choosing the ruler, disputes were probably inevitable.

When Muhammad died, the elders of the Medinese community chose Abu Bakr, one of the earliest converts, as *khalifah,* or successor—caliph in English. They bypassed Ali, Muhammad's cousin and son-in-law, who had the strongest claim based on kinship. Their decision caused disgruntlement among Ali's partisans, the *shiat Ali,* or Shiites, who believed that Ali had in fact been designated by Muhammad as his successor and that the office of caliph should be hereditary in the line of descent from Ali.

Ali was eventually selected as the fourth caliph, but by the time of his rule (656–661) the unity of the Muslim empire was already

Bernard Pierre Wolff

**Shiite Muslims in Lucknow, India, flagellating themselves**

breaking up. He was forced to defend his position against a challenge from other companions and associates of Muhammad. He prevailed in battle, but that branded him as the first caliph to lead Muslims in combat against other Muslims. Ali was then challenged by Muawiyah, the governor of Syria. Ali was assassinated, Muawiyah declared himself caliph and moved the seat of the office to Damascus, and in the year 680 routed an army led by Ali's son Husayn at Karbala, in Iraq. Shiite Muslims, who believed that Ali and his descendants were the rightful heirs to the prophet's spiritual authority, commemorate the "martyrdom" of Husayn with displays of public mourning and self-flagellation each year.

Those early engagements permanently shaped the history of Islam in three important ways:

First, they destroyed the unity of the brotherhood of the faithful and allowed power struggles and caliphal intrigues to become the political determinants of the empire. The office of caliph was dormant for centuries, though several Ottoman sultans and the Sharif of Mecca claimed it, and it was officially abolished in 1924 after the Kemalist revolution in Turkey. Rivalries among claimants to leadership in the world of Islam, however, continue.

Second, the struggle between Muawiyah and the family of Ali created a permanent division in the faith between the Shiites and the majority of Muslims who accepted the authority of the caliph. The majority are known as Sunnites, followers of the *sunna,* or way of the prophet. Shiites, partisans of Ali, believe that Ali and his descendants were divinely guided spiritual leaders called Imams. Sunnites have no central doctrinal authority. They adhere to practices and laws traceable by tradition to the words and deeds of the prophet, which are naturally open to differing interpretations. Shiism is the official creed in Iran and is also widespread in Iraq, Lebanon and Pakistan. About 15 percent of all Muslims are Shiites.

Third, the transfer of the caliphal seat to Damascus removed the center of Islamic power and of Islamic thought from the Arabian peninsula. In the 1,300 years since Muawiyah, the cultural capital of Islam has moved from Damascus to Baghdad to Cairo to Constantinople, and since the overthrow of the Ottoman sultans in Turkey after World War I, no city has been able to claim a position of intellectual or religious primacy in Islam. Islam has no Rome, no capital where historic and religious continuity holds the faith together. Islamic legitimacy thus has no geographical base; all Muslims face Mecca as they pray, and they go there on pilgrimage, but the sources of political and economic ideas and forms of artistic and intellectual expression are as diverse as the House of Islam itself.

## *Umayyad Downfall, Abbasid Triumph*

The Damascus dynasty of Muawiyah's Umayyad clan lasted less than a century, from 661 to 750, but it can be credited with two important achievements. One is the long succession of military conquests that carried the empire to its farthest limits and inevitably broadened Islam through exposure to and absorption of elements of Greek, Persian and Latin culture. The other is the development of an administrative system for the empire in which local officials and tax collectors were left in place even if they were not Muslims. The Umayyads built a government in what had been a patchwork of diverse territories seized almost haphazardly.

Insurrections in the provinces of the empire and internal feuding undermined their power, however, and they were overthrown by the Abbasids, a rival dynasty that originated in Iraq. (Even today Iraq and Syria remain hostile neighbors and political rivals. Both are Arab, both Muslim, and both ruled by branches of the Arab Baath Socialist party, but still they are at odds on every important issue.) The Abbasids defeated the Umayyad army, slew the caliph, moved the seat of the caliphate to a new capital at Baghdad, and began a long reign that marked the zenith of Islamic civilization.

At a time when Europe was mired in the Dark Ages, the Abbasid empire became the custodian of civilization, advancing in science and mathematics while preserving poetic and philosophical works in Greek, Syriac, Sanskrit and Persian. Under strong Persian influence, the Abbasid court was also a center of luxury and art. It was the court of *The Arabian Nights* legend. Muhammad and the early caliphs would hardly have recognized it as a center of Islam, which, while it does not teach asceticism, does teach restraint, discipline, and social behavior based on the prophet's example.

If ever there was a time when the ideal of the Islamic nation, a global, centralized self-perpetuating empire based on Islam, could have been realized, it was in the ninth century under the Abbasids. They had military power, vast wealth, cultural and scientific supremacy, and at least the appearance of religious legitimacy. But Islam failed to ensure political cohesion, just as it did before the Abbasids and just as it has done ever since.

The Abbasid empire died one of the most painful and lingering deaths of any in history. In name at least it endured for five centuries, until 1258, but its political fragmentation began while the caliph's power was still at its height. Corruption and indolence eroded the position of the caliphs and undercut their claims to be protectors of Islam. The caliph became a petty despot, dependent upon mercenary troops and professional bureaucrats to keep the state functioning. Turkish mercenaries imported to protect the court took it over, reducing the caliph to a puppet under their tutelage. In short, opportunism, corruption and political rivalry overcame the cohesive force of Islam. Entire provinces, while remaining loyal to the Muslim religion, broke away from caliphal rule. Rival Muslim dynasties arose in Turkey, North Africa and Oman, and even inside Iraq.

A North African Shiite dynasty called the Fatimids, after the prophet's daughter Fatima, built a capital at Cairo and quickly developed it into a new center of power and learning. In the east, the Seljuq Turks, who had been servants of the Baghdad court, ruled at Isfahan. In what remained of the Abbasid empire, allegiance to the caliph was often nominal.

When the Crusades began in 1095, the Abbasid caliph, still the theoretical protector of all Islam, was unable to rouse the remnants of empire to a unified response. The authority of Baghdad was further eroded as local princelings and crypto-caliphs made independent decisions about how to deal with the Christian invaders, and often accepted truces. The greatest Muslim military leader of the Crusades was not an Abbasid general but the sultan of Egypt, Saladin, who restored Jerusalem to Muslim control with a great victory over the Franks in 1187.

Thus the enfeebled Abbasids were unable to offer much resistance when the Mongol invasion swept out of the east in the 13th century. First under Genghis Khan, then under his grandson Hulagu, the Mongols pillaged Asia Minor, leveling cities and killing innocent citizens, on a campaign of destruction that has had few equals. Then in 1258 they laid seige to Baghdad.

It was an assault not just on a city but on an entire culture. When Baghdad fell, the Mongols murdered much of the Muslim population (sparing the non-Muslims), including the caliph and his family; they burned the schools and libraries and destroyed the mosques. The devastation put an end to Abbasid rule, to the great era of cultural and intellectual achievement in the Baghdad court, and to the primacy of Arabic civilization within Islam.

The faith itself survived. The rise of the Fatimids in Egypt and the leadership of Saladin had already moved the repository of the Islamic heritage to Cairo, which since 1250 had been ruled by the caste of slave-soldiers called Mamluks. When the Mongols tried to invade Egypt, they were defeated. The decisive battle was fought at Ain Jalut ("Spring of Goliath") in Palestine, in 1260. The battle, a landmark in Islamic history, is commemorated in the name of the Ain Jalut brigade, a unit of the Palestinian army in exile.

Islam by then was well-enough established and institutionalized not to be dependent for its existence on the survival of any one ruler or capital. For nearly three centuries, from the fall of Baghdad to the rise of the Ottoman Turks, petty dynasties proliferated throughout the Muslim world and no one power could claim to rule all Islam. The institutions of the faith, not those of army or government, provided stability and continuity in the community. Mosques, religious courts and schools, mystical brotherhoods and foundations financed by the zakat kept the Islamic community intact and preserved its sense of cohesion no matter which ruler seized the throne. In a broad sense the situation was similar to what exists today: a worldwide Muslim community prays together and performs the duties of the faith according to a shared belief, even as their rulers attack one another. Now as then, in times of trouble, it is natural for some groups to see an ideal in the basic, unequivocal rules and totally Islamic state as they existed in the time of Muhammad.

After the sack of Baghdad, Islam as a religion ceased to be in the intellectual vanguard of the world. As Europe emerged into the Renaissance, much of the Islamic world slipped into decline. Its military power was exhausted, and after the terror of the Mongols, the arbiters of the faith—teachers, religious judges, Koranic scholars—turned inward, perhaps in self-protection, and ceased to welcome new ideas. When the discovery of the New World and of new seaborne trade routes to the Far East cut off the European mercantile traffic that had traditionally moved across the caravan trails of the Middle East, it left the heartland of Islam both impoverished and culturally isolated. Powerful and splendid

Islamic empires later arose in Persia and India, but for most of the House of Islam, those conditions would prevail until the Arab nationalist wave broke over the Levant in the 19th century.

## Ottoman Empire (c. 1683)

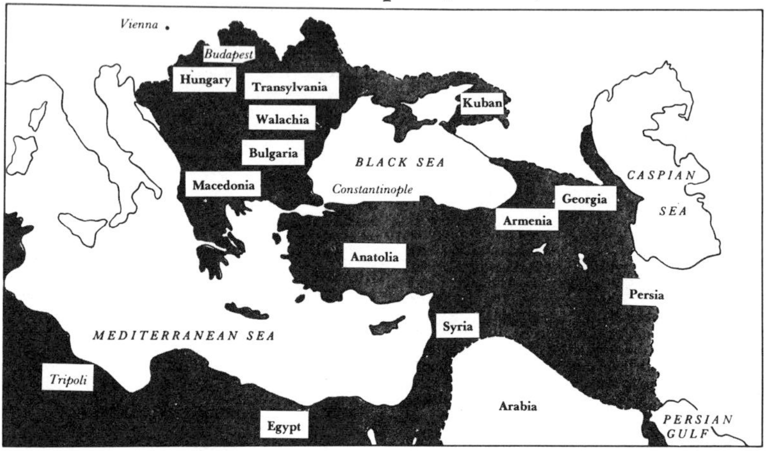

[Map showing the Ottoman Empire c. 1683, with labels: Vienna, Budapest, Hungary, Transylvania, Walachia, Kuban, Bulgaria, Macedonia, Constantinople, BLACK SEA, Georgia, Armenia, CASPIAN SEA, Anatolia, Persia, MEDITERRANEAN SEA, Syria, Tripoli, Arabia, Egypt, PERSIAN GULF]

From *The Columbia Encyclopedia*, 4th ed. Columbia University Press, 1975. Reprinted with permission.

At the height of Ottoman power, under Suleiman the Magnificent, 1520–66, Turkish rule imposed a measure of unity on a part of the Muslim world and even brought capital improvements such as waterworks and canals to such outposts as Jerusalem, Mecca, and Basra, in Iraq. But the Turks, though Muslims, were still foreign occupiers in the Islamic heartland of the Middle East and Egypt. Under their imperial rule, the glorious achievements of the 16th century quickly gave way to decline, and living conditions in Arabia and North Africa sank into squalor and poverty for most people. Among the ruling classes, the Turks extracted loyalty by force, and they imposed their own bureaucratic system; but Ottoman rule remained an imperial occupation, not a genuine Islamic unity, and as the Ottomans spent their energies on struggles with the Persians to the east and with European rivals in the Balkans, the Ottoman empire followed the pattern of the Abbasids.

As the nominal sovereign of all the Islamic countries west of

Persia except Morocco, the Ottoman sultan was responsible for the defense of the faith and the protection of the holy places of Islam. It was the Turkish ruler who in 1811 dispatched an Egyptian army under Muhammad Ali to retake Mecca and Medina after they had been seized by the puritanical Wahhabi sect led by the house of Saud, which continues to rule Saudi Arabia. (Then as now, fundamentalism challenged the political power of the ruler.) By the 19th century, however, the Sublime Porte (a common synonym for Ottoman rule) was so enfeebled that the outlying provinces of the Ottoman empire were beyond real Turkish control; the Wahhabis could be put down, but the sultan could no longer prevent European encroachment into Iraq, the Levant, North Africa and southern Arabia.

When Napoleon Bonaparte invaded Egypt in 1798, the strength of Europe and the weakness of the Muslim people were shockingly apparent. The French troops brushed aside the Mamluk cavalry, and the scholars who accompanied the expedition introduced the first Arabic printing press the Egyptians had ever seen. A new era in Islamic history began: the era of European colonialism. From Dutch-ruled Indonesia to French-ruled Morocco, the impoverished, enfeebled and culturally backward Muslim countries fell under European economic, military and administrative domination.

The Europeans carved up the territory and imposed national boundaries that overrode traditional allegiances: the boundaries of Somalia, Iraq, Libya, Lebanon and other states (including, of course, the British-mandated territory of Palestine) were drawn by European powers. The Europeans brought new ideas about science, urban development, technology, navigation, law and political organization. Young Arab men went to European universities and got their military training from European officers. At the same time, deep Arab resentment against Turkish domination inspired a nationalist movement that arose in Syria and Lebanon and spread rapidly; even in territories where arrangements between the Turks and their European rivals left Turkish rule nominally in place, Arab opposition to the Turks was undermining what remained of the Ottoman empire.

At the outbreak of World War I, the last Ottoman sultan commanded all Muslims to support the Sublime Porte and its ally Germany against France, Britain and Russia. This was the last serious attempt by any Muslim ruler to enlist the faithful in a campaign based on religion, and it was an utter failure. Led by Husayn, the Sharif of Mecca, the Arabs of the Hejaz spurned the sultan and supported the British—not because of any love for the British and French but because of their desire to be independent of Turkish rule and their belief that Britain and France would give them independence after the war.

The Arabs put their nationalist aspirations ahead of their religious loyalty. In doing so they followed a pattern that is traceable to Islam's first century and still prevails. The fraternity of the Islamic religion, strong among individuals, does not override political considerations or nationalist ambitions among groups and governments. It is only necessary to consider the current relations between Iran and Iraq, Egypt and Libya or Algeria and Morocco to realize that Islam has little unifying power on a transnational basis.

The Arabs' support for Britain, France and Russia in World War I turned out to be misplaced, because the European powers betrayed them. Even before the war was over, they arranged, in the Sykes-Picot Agreement, to carve up the former Ottoman territories between them instead of giving the Arabs their independence. That agreement, and the 1917 Balfour Declaration, in which Britain pledged to support "the establishment in Palestine of a national home for the Jewish people," and the colonial experience of Algeria, Libya and Pakistan, created the setting for much of the political turbulence that has afflicted the Islamic world in this century.

The colonial or imperialist era ended the isolation and intellectual stagnation in which the Muslim world had lived for so long, but it also created conditions in which extremism and violence can flourish. Most Muslim countries, independent only for a generation or two, are still searching for an appropriate and durable form of government. Hardly any, except possibly Saudi Arabia and Kuwait, have succeeded in creating political systems assured of surviving the death or ouster of the present ruler. At the same time, they are groping for social formulas and educational systems that would give them material progress without materialism, Western technology without Western domination, and cultural continuity without isolation.

Those are difficult passages in the life of any nation. In the Muslim world they are made especially difficult by economic conditions—immense overnight wealth in Saudi Arabia and Libya, crushing poverty in Somalia and Egypt; by great-power rivalries—pro-Soviet Libya against U.S.-ally Egypt, Soviet-dominated Afghanistan confronting pro-Western Pakistan; and by the lingering geographic and ethnic rivalries arising from artificial state boundaries imposed in the imperalist era.

Any of these volatile issues could create fertile ground for religious extremism, or at least for a movement to make Islam the dominant consideration in setting policy. An Islamic group that espouses the establishment of Islamic law in place of European systems, the retaking of some piece of turf excised from the historic homeland by Western powers, and neutralism in place of great-power allegiances might well appear "extremist" to those whose interests are threatened by such a program. In the context of societies seeking to reassert their political and cultural independence, however, such a group might well have a natural appeal. Viewed from the perspective of people who are poor, disenfranchised, or trying to protect their traditions against the shock of change, movements and ideas that appear extreme and irrational to Westerners are both logical and acceptable.

# 3

# The Key Countries

***IRAN***

The Iranian revolution brought to power a deeply conservative, xenophobic and absolutist government dominated by religious elders of the Shiite branch of Islam.

In its virulent anti-Americanism, reactionary social policies and Jacobin-like zeal to purge suspected enemies, the Iranian regime appears as the ultimate menace of militant Islam to Western ideals and interests.

It is not at all clear, however, that the Iranian revolution has run its course and the present system will be the one that ultimately emerges; even if the present form of revolutionary government stays in power, it does not necessarily represent a model that other Muslim societies are likely to emulate. As Professor Michael C. Hudson of Georgetown University has written, "The Iranian revolution, of course, is the preeminent example of a successful Islamic opposition movement. It is also the only example."

Muslim fundamentalism and religious reaction are hardly unique to Iran. They have existed in Egypt and other Muslim countries for decades without succeeding in moving from the political fringes to the mainstream, and it cannot be assumed that events in Iran will alter the situation elsewhere.

Nor is it a given that doctrinaire religious regimes that impose traditional Koranic social and legal patterns on their countries will necessarily be hostile to Western strategic interests. The examples of Pakistan and Saudi Arabia show otherwise.

Furthermore, many of the conditions that led to the triumph of the Iranian revolution were unique to that country. Iran is the only nation where Shiism is the predominant and official creed. Shiites believe that the line of succession to Muhammad passed to Ali, then to Ali's son Husayn, and then down through a line of divinely guided Imams, all descendants of Ali, who were both temporal and spiritual leaders of the Muslim community. The 12th Imam disappeared into "occultation" or a hidden state in the ninth century, but he is still alive and will return one day to preside over a perfected society, Iranian Shiites believe.

No person visible today actually claims to be the returned Imam. Ayatollah Khomeini, the Iranian leader, is referred to as Imam, but it is an honorary title. But the idea, the concept of the Imamate creates in Shiite society an inclination to accept the moral leadership of an individual. Khomeini's position as spiritual guide and de facto ruler probably could only have developed in a Shiite society conditioned to the acceptance of ecclesiastical authority. Only Iran had the network of powerful mullahs and ayatollahs that collectively represented an approximation of the Imamate.

In other Muslim countries, where Sunnites predominate, there is no comparable religious figure. The Sunni leadership is generally a co-opted creature of the state, which controls the mosques, universities and religious posts, and therefore the religious elders are not in a position to encourage dissent. In fact, as Professor Hudson has pointed out, in countries other than Iran "the very emasculation of the government-dominated Islamic establishment opens the way for opposition movements to bid for Islamic legitimacy."

That is what has happened in Egypt, where the senior religious figure, the Grand Shayk of Al-Azhar mosque and university, is a

United Press International Photo

**Teheran, March 19, 1979: Iranian soldiers, in their first parade after the revolution, demonstrate their support for Ayatollah Khomeini.**

presidential appointee. The most extreme religious groups have counted the country's prominent religious leaders among their targets.

## *EGYPT*

The modern history of organized, fundamentalist religious agitation in Egypt can be traced to 1928, the year of the founding of the Muslim Brotherhood. Egypt was then the most Europeanized of Islamic societies, and it had been fertile ground for the secular modernists and reformers who liberated Muslim religious thinking in the late 19th and early 20th centuries.

Nominally independent at least in domestic affairs, Egypt was actually under British domination, which a nationalist uprising in 1919 had failed to shake. Though famous patriots such as Saad Zaghlul had agitated for true independence, conventional bourgeois politics was doing little either to achieve Egyptian nationalist goals or to improve the lives of the illiterate masses. By Western standards the society was deeply conservative, but by the standards of Hassan al-Banna it was corrupt, materialistic and compromised—and therefore un-Islamic.

Banna, a schoolteacher, founded the Muslim Brotherhood and was its "supreme guide" until he was murdered in 1949. He was a deeply religious and devout man who was distressed by what he saw as Egypt's social corruption and the erosion of Islamic traditions. Secular education, the unveiling of women, imported legal systems, bickering political parties with programs built only on pragmatism, all seemed to him manifestations of a nationwide erosion of Islam. He preached piety and virtue to bands of zealous young followers, cooking up a volatile mix of religion and nationalism that led almost inevitably to extremist methods. He saw himself as a religious reformer; he demanded an end to Western domination, a purge of alien cultural influences and the establishment of a government based on Koranic principles.

The Brotherhood had widespread appeal among the poorer classes—workers, impoverished students, peasants—who were least tainted by Western influence and had the least to lose in a confrontation with the established system. Though no firm figures on membership have ever been published, informed estimates put the number at about half a million during the period of the Brotherhood's greatest power, the late 1940s. The influence of the Muslim Brothers spread well beyond their own ranks, however, because they were extremely well organized. They had cells everywhere, in factories, trade unions and universities, and they ran several successful businesses, including their own publishing house. They also had camps where members underwent paramilitary training.

Their rising power and their relentless demands for a total Islamization of Egyptian life threatened the conventional politicians, and in December 1948 Prime Minister Mahmoud Nuqrashi provoked a confrontation. He ordered the dissolution of the Brotherhood and a ban on its activities. Shortly thereafter one of the Brothers murdered Nuqrashi. Then on February 12, 1949, Banna was killed, probably by government agents.

## *The Nasser Revolution*

With the monarchy tottering and the bourgeois political parties mired in sterile bickering, the Brothers stepped up the campaign of bombings and assassinations that earned them their reputation as terrorists. But when revolution came to Egypt in 1952, it was not they who carried it out. It was the Association of Free Officers, a movement within the army led by Gamal Abdel Nasser and a few associates, including Sadat. Years earlier, the Free Officers had rejected a proffered alliance with the Brotherhood—Sadat was the liaison man with Banna—because the officers' program was nationalistic, not religious. When they came to power, the Brotherhood turned on them.

Nasser and his compatriots established a regime that was neither religious nor xenophobic and made no attempt to impose puritanical standards of behavior on Egyptian society. As a result, the Muslim Brothers attempted to assassinate Nasser in 1954, and he responded as firmly as possible: six leaders of the Brotherhood were hanged and about a thousand imprisoned, some to remain locked up until after Nasser's death 16 years later. The Brotherhood attempted to regroup as a clandestine movement in the mid-1960s, and Nasser rounded up thousands more members and imprisoned them too.

After Sadat succeeded Nasser in 1970, he gradually lifted the curbs on the Brotherhood. Technically the organization remained illegal but until the month before his death Sadat permitted it to function semipublicly, organize prayer meetings, publish a magazine and recruit members.

Despite their fearsome reputation, the Brothers were a fairly tame group under Sadat. They existed on the sufferance of the government; and while they often opposed Sadat's policies, especially his peace with Israel and his support for the shah of Iran, they refrained from violence.

Other countries, especially Syria and Algeria, have blamed the Brotherhood for recent violence, but it is not clear that so-called Muslim Brotherhoods outside Egypt are linked to the original organization. In the 1940s, the Egyptian Brotherhood had branches in several other countries, the largest in Syria. The current Syrian government has blamed the Muslim Brotherhood for the long series of assassinations and bombings that have plagued the regime of President Hafez al-Assad. In Algeria, the government held a branch of the Brotherhood responsible for an outbreak of extremist violence in late 1981. Algeria's Superior Islamic Council accused the Brotherhood of "distorting the teachings of Islam, spreading a false faith, inciting disorders and desecrating a holy place." Neither the Syrians nor the Algerians, however, made public much credible evidence that would link the extremist groups in their countries to the original Egyptian Brotherhood. It is possible that local organizations have adopted the name because of what it stands for in the history of fundamentalist political movements.

On September 5, 1981, just a month before he was slain, Sadat announced a new crackdown on the Brotherhood and on other groups in the Egyptian opposition, including other religious groups, which he said were fomenting religious strife and promoting violence in Egypt. "The Muslim Brotherhood, as an association, does not exist officially and is illegal," he said. The decision of Nasser's old Revolutionary Command Council to suppress the Brotherhood was still in effect, he said, and "therefore there is no association and it has no right to even publish a journal."

By that time, however, the Brotherhood had long since yielded its position on the violent fringe of the religious extremist movement to the shadowy, reckless gang known as Takfir Wahigra (literally Takfir wa al-Hijra, or Atonement and Migration Society), the group originally suspected of carrying out Sadat's assassination and probably responsible for disorders that followed in the town of Asyut.

Takfir Wahigra is a true fringe group, deliberately putting itself outside the mainstream of society. Unlike the Brothers, who infiltrated and took over conventional institutions in their effort to Islamicize society, Takfir Wahigra taught that Egyptian society was so corrupt it had to be abandoned altogether; the organization encourages its members to leave home—to migrate to communal settlements that would be the foundation of a purged nation.

The group was founded by a zealot named Shukri Ahmed

Mustafa, an agronomist from Asyut, who had been a Muslim Brother and was among those rounded up by Nasser in 1966. Released in the general amnesty that followed Sadat's accession to the presidency, he split with the Brotherhood, apparently because he regarded it as compromised, and found it necessary to impose his absolutist religious views through violence.

In 1974 the gang staged an armed attack on the Military Technical College near Cairo, apparently as part of a plan to assassinate Sadat. Some of the participants in that incident were still in jail when the group struck again two years later. Members of Takfir Wahigra kidnapped and executed Shaykh Muhammad Zahabi, a former minister of religious affairs who was a pillar of the traditional religious establishment and a prominent critic of extremist cults. The group let it be known that the murder was planned as the start of an uprising against what they saw as an immoral and corrupt system of law and government and against a religious establishment that in their view had abandoned Islamic principles.

Shukri Mustafa and four of his followers were arrested not long after the killing and were promptly hanged. At the time those measures appeared to put an end to the Takfir Wahigra menace; Shukri Mustafa had told police the group had some 4,000 members, but it never had the broad-based appeal or organizational ability that the Muslim Brotherhood had, and the elimination of its leaders was thought to end its activities. Some of those seized in Sadat's last crackdown, however, were said to be members. When Sadat was killed, Egyptian authorities indicated that members of the group were still at large and might have been responsible, though it appears that the assassination was the work of a small, extremist group inside the army that had no overall program, only a deep hostility to Sadat's rule.

### *Conservative Islamic Groups*

Islamic militancy and fundamentalism do not always take the form of violent protest. Also active in Egypt, especially on university campuses, and much larger in membership, are scores of Islamic associations, loosely structured but ideologically linked,

Bernard Pierre Wolff
**Veiled women in the northern Indian city of Varanasi**

that espouse a conservative religious program. These Islamic associations, with names like Muhammad's Youth, first attracted notice in the mid-1970s when their male members grew beards and their women put on full-length, monochromatic dresses and even, in a few cases, the veil. They favor Koran-based government and they oppose the cultural inroads of the West represented by such events as campus rock concerts. They have even sought segregation by sex in medical school classes. In general they are nonviolent, but their sheer numbers, visibility and persistence will require any Egyptian government either to make some concessions to them or to repress them.

## *TURKEY*

Ever since the Kemalist revolution of 1922, it has been official policy in Turkey to subordinate Islam to Turkish nationalism as the guiding principle of the country, to excise religion from government and politics, and to sever Turkey from Islam's Arabic heritage through such measures as a ban on the Arabic script and the use of Turkish translations in Koran readings.

Mustafa Kemal Ataturk, the father of modern Turkey, was determined to take his country out of the Orient and convert it into a European state, which meant adopting Western ways in law, education, social policy and even dress. He banned the wearing of the fez and other brimless headgear, shocking Muslim men who had adopted such caps so they could put their foreheads to the floor in prayer without uncovering their heads. The state took over education; religious schools and courts were abolished. Public displays of worship were discouraged, and the role of Islam in public ceremonies and on the radio was curtailed.

But Turkey remains a Muslim society, and as a republic characterized by free-swinging electoral politics interspersed with military takeover, the country has had to make some compromises with popular sentiment. According to historian Martin Kramer, author of "Political Islam," a Georgetown University study, both the principal conservative party, the Justice party, and its predecessor, the Democratic party, "began to appreciate the political benefits that accrued from inclusion of Islamic planks in their platforms."

For some time the compromises on Islamic issues were relatively minor. The call to prayer was permitted to be recited in Arabic, for example. But in the 1970s there appeared a full-scale political movement advocating a return to the Islamic state. This was the National Salvation party (NSP) led by Necmettin Erbakan.

Led by technocrats rather than by professional religious figures, the party nonetheless espoused a familiar program based on religious ideals: limitations on alcohol, a ban on the "defamation" of Islam, the return of religious education to the schools. Erbakan even suggested that shari'ah might again have a place in Turkish life, an idea that challenged the Constitution.

Despite evidence of growing religious consciousness and pride among the Turkish people, however, the NSP has not been successful at the polls. In the mid-1970s, when popular demonstrations of religious sentiment were on the rise, the party's appeal diminished. It captured 11.8 percent of the popular vote in 1973 but only 8.6 percent in 1977.

Journalist G. H. Jansen, in his book *Militant Islam*, offers a persuasive explanation for the failure of the NSP and the National Action party, which also appeals to Islamic sentiment, to gain popular support. Both, he says, are "merely using the religion for essentially political and nonreligious purposes... Despite their crude appeals to popular Islamic feeling, neither party has as yet been able to rally widespread support, which is to the credit of Turkish Islam." In a prescient political prediction, Jansen said that if the Turkish armed forces "tire once again of the self-seeking game of the politicians and retake power, then, in the name of the secular Kemalist 'revolution,' they will apply the brakes to any movement toward Islamic politics, genuine or otherwise."

That was exactly what happened. In 1980, after a mass rally staged by Erbakan in which men wearing turbans and brandishing signs in the banned Arabic script demanded an end to secularism, the armed forces seized power to put an end to the country's political chaos and violence. The generals vowed to take religion out of politics and put it back where it belonged, in the mosque.

## *TUNISIA*

Tunisia, since it gained independence from France in 1956, has been among the most relaxed, secular and Europeanized of the Muslim countries. To cross from Libya into neighboring Tunisia is to pass from a harsh and austere world of religious absolutism and Arab nationalism into a relaxed environment of French-accented easy living, secular government, and scantily clad tourists on the beaches. The liberal atmosphere was bound to offend religious traditionalists; even nonreligious intellectuals were uncomfortable with the implications of the arrival of bare-breasted European women on beaches adjacent to traditional villages.

Under the leadership of Habib Bourguiba, its only president since independence, Tunisia has adopted a social code more liberal than that of almost any other Muslim country: polygamy is prohibited, women are permitted to institute divorce proceedings and serve in the army, Koranic schools have been nationalized, and most of the powers of the religious courts have been transferred to civil tribunals.

In that atmosphere it was probably inevitable that an opposition movement should arise based on conservative Islamic ideals and Arab nationalism. Trade unionists who found prosperity elusive and students who were restive under Tunisia's one-party system were a natural constituency for the Mouvement de Tendance Islamique (MTI), which became an active opposition force in the late 1970s and challenged the government directly in 1981.

Led by two fiery orators, Rashid Ghannouchi, a Tunis University professor, and Abdelfattah Mourou, a lawyer, the fundamentalists kept up a months-long barrage of criticism of government policies. One group of students issued a proclamation saying, "We are a social, educational and cultural movement, working to stir up this society to recover its deep Muslim roots and to spread Islamic culture."

Then the agitators exceeded the limits the government was prepared to tolerate. In June 1981, several hundred zealots raided a Club Mediterranée resort, denouncing the freewheeling lifestyle of its swimsuit-clad guests and accusing the club of Zionist connections because it also operates resorts in Israel. That direct attack on the tourism industry, a mainstay of the economy, took the movement out of the mosques and lecture halls into direct confrontation with the government. Scores of participants were arrested.

On September 4, 1981, a court in Tunis imposed jail terms ranging from six months to 11 years. Ghannouchi got 11 years, Mourou, 10. But those measures will probably not put an end to the MTI or to the views it represents. The forces that generated it are still at work in Tunisia, and the country's position as seat of the Arab League, which moved its headquarters there from Cairo after Sadat's peace treaty with Israel, has reportedly sensitized it to Arab issues. When Bourguiba, who is old and ailing, finally yields control, the religious movement is likely to be one of the bidders for power.

## *PAKISTAN*

Unlike such countries as Egypt and Iraq, which have centuries of pre-Islamic history, Pakistan was created as an Islamic state. It was carved out of British India as a separate state for Muslims at the time of independence in 1947.

Pakistan then consisted of two parts, East and West, separated by more than 1,000 miles of India. East Pakistan became the independent nation of Bangladesh after the 1971 civil war. It is today the second-largest Muslim nation in population, after Indonesia, but because of its small land area, its poverty and its isolation, it commands relatively little attention in the West.

Pakistan, on the other hand, is one of the key Muslim states in U.S. strategic planning. Traditionally friendly with the United States despite strong differences over such issues as nuclear weapons development, Pakistan has maintained a close military relationship with the United States, and its safety became a matter of urgent concern when the Soviet Union invaded neighboring Afghanistan at the end of 1979.

Though created as a Muslim state whose Constitution calls for "the reconstruction of Muslim society on a truly Islamic basis," Pakistan has never succeeded in defining for itself what that means in practice, what kind of government it should have or to what extent the rules of religion, such as payment of the zakat, should be enforced by the state.

In the 1970s, the government of Prime Minister Zulfikar Ali Bhutto was relatively flexible on religious issues, but it faced constant agitation from religiously oriented political parties demanding full Islamization of the state.

President Muhammad Zia ul-Haq, who seized power from Bhutto in a military coup in 1977, has chosen the course that Bhutto and his predecessors resisted: full unity of religion and state policy, with the laws, social system and educational principles of the nation built on Koranic rules and religious tradition.

This program has been easier to proclaim than to implement, partly because of disagreements between the country's Sunnite majority and large Shiite minority over such issues as mandatory state collection of the zakat, which Shiites oppose.

Zia's program is as much nationalistic as religious. The substitution of Arabic for English as the first foreign language taught in the schools, for example, is dictated by the desire to read the Koran in the original, but there are no religious reasons for requiring government workers to abandon suits and neckties in favor of native-style pantaloons and tunics. Zia has imposed such obvious measures as a ban on alcohol, mandatory observance of prayer-time in the workplace, abolition of banking interest and restoration of Koranic punishments for some crimes, but he has not been able to achieve a nationwide consensus in support of either his religious or his political policies.

Zia rules largely by decree, and he has used religion as a means of legitimizing his presidency. He gave prestigious positions in the government to members of the most prominent religious party, the fundamentalist Jamaat-i-Islami, thus co-opting the religious opposition, and he focused on religious issues to establish himself as arbiter of the faith. After five years of rule he has still not committed himself as to the form of government he envisions for an Islamic state. He appointed a 288-member Advisory Council and described it as "an intermediary stage between the martial law government and the future Islamic democratic government," without specifying what the latter might consist of.

Pakistan's religious regimen is in place because Zia imposed it, not because there is a clear national consensus on the form and function of an Islamic state, which there never has been. It is not at all certain that a successor regime would follow the same path. Zia's problem, and Pakistan's, is that the religious measures have done nothing to address the fundamental and enduring problems of the country: poverty, overpopulation, ethnic divisions, regional separatist agitation and military weakness.

## *AFGHANISTAN*

The situation in Afghanistan is unique. Several groups of rebels, motivated partly by religion and partly by nationalist patriotism, are conducting a guerrilla war and campaign of sabotage against the Soviet troops who occupied Afghanistan in December 1979 and the puppet government they installed.

The insurgency began, however, more than a year before the Soviet invasion. It was a rebellion against the indigenous Marxist regime of Nur Muhammad Taraki and Hafizullah Amin that seized power in a coup in April 1978. That government, leftist in program and irreligious in style, provoked opposition among the traditionally unruly herdsmen and farmers in the hills and among groups of better-educated exiles living mostly across the Khyber Pass in Peshawar, Pakistan. The Soviet invasion, in which Amin was killed, only increased the determination of the rebels, because the government of Babrak Karmal is just as leftist and atheist as the one it replaced, and it holds power only because of the Soviet military presence.

Karmal begins his speeches with the standard Muslim invocation, "In the name of God, the merciful, the compassionate." In his first address to the nation, on December 27, 1979, he pledged that his government would "respect the sacred principles of Islam, freedom of conscience, belief and religious rites." But the rebels had heard the same thing from predecessor regimes, and they were not placated.

At least six separate exile groups, all professing religious motivation, claim to be leading the rebellion. The two most prominent, which maintain highly visible offices in Peshawar, are the Hezb-i-Islami, or Islamic party, headed by Gulbuddin Hekmatyar, a former engineering student, and the Jamaat-i-Islami, or Islamic Society, headed by Burhanuddin Rabbani, a former professor of Islamic theology at Kabul University.

The groups have similar programs. They want to oust the Soviets, get rid of the Marxist government in Kabul, end the state's assault on religious institutions and on local customs, and establish an Islamic republic in which Islam would be the political determinant of the state.

As anti-Soviet Muslim organizations, these groups receive some assistance from other Muslim countries, but their campaign has been undermined by their own rivalry. Reports from inside Afghanistan in 1980 said the rebels were fighting each other as often as they were fighting government troops or the Soviets. A Dutch journalist who spent three weeks with the rebels in the spring of 1980 reported sustained gun battles between rebel groups that left hundreds dead.

In 1981 the rebels announced an agreement to settle their differences and combine their resources to fight their common enemy, but the reports from Afghanistan about whether they have succeeded are scanty and inconclusive.

## *SAUDI ARABIA*

In the first century of Islam, the Arabian peninsula was the motherland of the faith, the society on which the religion's teachings were based, the source of its language and of its ideals. In this century Saudi Arabia, though newly unified, backward, isolated and until recently impoverished, has reemerged as the self-proclaimed guardian of the Islamic conscience and the arbiter of Muslim values. That is the result of the unique partnership in power of the Royal House of Saud and the religious reformers of the Wahhabi movement.

Roughly speaking, Wahhabism is to Islam as Puritanism is to Christianity: a back-to-basics reform movement aimed at purging the faith of corrupt influences and ritual excesses and at building a community based on the Koran. The movement takes its name from Muhammad ibn Abd al-Wahhab, a legal scholar and Islamic jurist, who was born in central Arabia in 1703.

Though trained in an orthodox legal school, he also had early experience as a Sufi, or Muslim mystic. Fraternal mystical orders espousing a personal and emotional knowledge of God have existed within Islam for centuries. Abd al-Wahhab blamed the weakness of the Muslim community on the results of Sufi excesses. Revulsion against such practices as initiation rituals and the use of music in religious ceremonies stimulated Abd al-Wahhab to a reform campaign.

Though in the contemporary world the Wahhabis are often thought of as reactionaries, Wahhabism was in fact a liberating force in Muslim intellectual history. The Wahhabis, though literalist in interpreting the Koran, nonetheless reopened the way for individual assessment of what it said. By insisting on the Koran as the only text and its rules as the only rules, they broke away from the convoluted and sterile analogical reasoning of the medieval legists.

In the mid-1740s, Abd al-Wahhab formed an alliance with Muhammad ibn Saud, a leader of a prominent central Arabian family, and began to impose his views by military action. When Muhammad ibn Saud died, he was succeeded by a skillful warrior named Abdul-Aziz ibn Saud, ancestor and namesake of the first king of modern Saudi Arabia.

The Wahhabis marched out of central Arabia into western Arabia and Iraq. They captured Mecca and Medina and sacked the tomb of the Shiite patriarch Husayn at Karbala. They forced the Ottoman governor of Baghdad to accept an armistice and then invaded Syria.

These gains obliged the Ottoman sultan to respond. As nominal ruler of the Islamic empire and as "protector of the holy places," he had to confront the political and military challenge of the Wahhabis, regardless of the merit of their doctrinal views. In 1811 he persuaded his viceroy in Egypt, Muhammad Ali, the "great modernizer" who took over Egypt after Napoleon withdrew and built the modern Egyptian state, to undertake an expedition against the Wahhabis.

It took seven years, but the result was a total victory for Muhammad Ali's forces. The sultan's nominal rule over Mecca and Medina was restored, the Saudi leader executed and Wahhabism confined to its place of origin, the oasis towns of central Arabia. The Saudis lost even those strongholds in a conflict with a rival clan late in the 19th century. The Saudi princes were exiled to Kuwait in 1891, and it appeared that Wahhabism would retreat into the history books as other sects had done before it.

### *Wahhabi Resurgence*

In 1902, however, a young prince of the exiled family, Abdul-Aziz ibn Saud, returned from Kuwait, and with a raiding party of only 40 men retook the town of his ancestors, Riyadh. From that base, the Wahhabis resumed their campaign to take control of the Arabian peninsula. World War I created the conditions that enabled them to succeed.

In that conflict the Saudis' rival, Husayn, the Sharif of Mecca, ignored an appeal from the Ottoman sultan for Arab support. Hoping for Arab independence after the war, he cast his lot with the British, and the Arabs rose against the Ottomans in the celebrated desert guerrilla campaign led by British officers, including T. E. Lawrence.

At the end of the war, however, Husayn's position was weak. The British and French undercut him with the Sykes-Picot Agreement and the Balfour Declaration. Then when the Turkish revolutionaries abolished the caliphate, he made an ill-advised attempt to claim it for himself, which was ridiculed by other Muslims. Thus Husayn had neither the protection of the Turks nor the rewards of his support for the British nor his own integrity intact, and when the Wahhabis renewed their campaign he was able to offer little resistance.

The Wahhabis were dedicated, ascetic warriors from a harsh environment, organized by Abdul-Aziz into armed brotherhoods fired by puritanical zeal. They took Mecca in October 1924, then Jiddah a year later. In 1926, Abdul-Aziz was proclaimed king of the Hejaz, or western Arabia. Within ten years he had unified the tribes into what is now the Kingdom of Saudi Arabia and imposed on them the puritanical and austere principles of Wahhabism, the ideological and social foundation of the kingdom.

The House of Saud and the principles of Wahhabi Islam rule Saudi Arabia today. Islam is the country's constitution, its law, its guide to social organization and public policy. Abdul-Aziz forced the reactionary elders of the faith to accept the principle that technological advancement and material modernization are accepted by the Koran; Islam provides the rules by which the society judges itself as that modernization takes place.

Saudi Arabia claims to be a true Islamic state. Unlike Pakistan and Libya, where the national relationship between Islam and the state is defined by one man—a military ruler who seized power and sought to legitimize his coup by religion—the Saudi system has so far been a durable partnership of ruling family, tribe and religion.

Islam is the foundation of the House of Saud. The Saudis,

through their puritanism and their nationalism, have restored Arabian primacy within the religion. They have given political and financial support to Muslim causes and movements around the world. Yet even they are not immune to criticism.

The Koran says Muslims should "conduct their affairs by mutual consultation." Many modern scholars have taken that to mean that a true Islamic government must be a republic, at least in form, as in revolutionary Iran. The Saudis say their informal system of consultations among rulers, religious leaders and the public is truly democratic; but by banning political parties, labor unions and any type of formal representative government they have exposed themselves to the criticism that their form of Islamic state is actually un-Islamic. (On the other hand, some Muslim authorities argue that it is the republican form of government that is un-Islamic: it implies legislation, when Islam teaches that all law comes from God.)

It is extremely difficult to gauge the extent of political opposition to the Saudi regime. The country is so vast—four times the size of France—and so sparsely populated, with only about 7 million residents, that it lacks the teeming urban centers and industrial concentrations which breed dissent. A potential trouble spot, the oil installations of the eastern province where there is a large Shiite population, has been the scene of some agitation, but it is of course closely watched, by the Saudis and by the United States.

Entry into Saudi Arabia is controlled, security measures are thorough, the press docile; and the government, while embarrassed by some spectacular incidents of corruption, can rightly claim that it has expended uncountable billions of its oil revenues on improved roads, schools, water supplies, housing and medical care for the population. Unlike Egypt and Pakistan, Saudi Arabia really is a land of opportunity, where a young man who goes to school can quickly achieve a style of living that was beyond the imagination of his parents. No bands of jobless students haunt the cafés.

The one serious challenge to the ruling system since the founding of the state in 1932 was religiously based, and it caught the government by surprise. In late 1979, a gang of several hundred armed men seized and occupied the most sacred shrine of Islam, the Great Mosque of Mecca. As James Piscatori of Britain's Royal Institute of International Affairs said in an essay on Saudi politics, this action "presented both a direct political challenge to the government in the example of open armed rebellion and an indirect but no less real political challenge by suggesting that the Sauds might not be so dependable after all as protectors of the holy places."

The Koran prohibits the shedding of blood at the holy shrine. The occupiers, by violating that taboo, opened themselves to retaliation. The government, however, took the precaution of obtaining a *fatwa* or religious decree from the Muslim elders before authorizing security forces to storm the mosque.

The government acted, in effect, as the agent of Islam in retaking the mosque by force and in executing some of the men who were captured. The action reaffirmed the partnership of Islam and the House of Saud, enhancing at least briefly the legitimacy of the regime after it had been embarrassed by the incident. It turned out that many of the occupiers were not Saudis: they included Palestinians, Pakistanis, Egyptians and Yemenis who were apparently affiliated with Takfir Wahigra. Thus the incident was not necessarily indicative of dissent within the Saudi body politic itself.

### *Islam's Many Mansions*

To these brief outlines could be added others dealing with major Muslim nations that are of less immediate concern to the United States: Indonesia, where the government and religion have maintained an uneasy truce for years; Malaysia, which is searching for legal and social formulas acceptable to the Muslim half of the population and to the non-Muslim half; and Nigeria, the biggest and richest country in sub-Saharan Africa, where about half the 80 million people are Muslims, and the government is obliged to deal with periodic outbreaks of religious turbulence.

In each there are groups and individuals who assert the

primacy of Islam and who would impose Islamic laws and principles on the entire society. But they cannot be grouped more closely than that for the purpose of seeing a worldwide wave of Muslim fundamentalism. In ethnic composition, colonial background, and regional strategic position, they are so different that events in one cannot be relevant to events in another. Unlike Turkey, Iran and the Arab states, which have common threads in their history that predate Islam, the outlying states of the world of Islam are largely insulated from each other and from the volcanic politics of the Middle East. Their people are part of the House of Islam and any generalized, global threat to the faith would of course involve them; absent that, their political development ought not to be considered in the same framework as events in Iran or Egypt. Especially isolated are the estimated 45 million Muslims in the Soviet Union, who continue to practice their faith to some extent but are cut off from the unifying and sustaining contacts of the pilgrimage. Though the Soviet authorities have tolerated the existence of a few mosques, they have organized the army, the educational system and the political structure in such a way as to undermine the perpetuation of the Islamic religion as a separate political force.

# 4

# Lessons for Policy-makers

When Egypt and Syria were preparing to go to war against Israel in 1973, they code-named the attack "Operation Badr." The name and its symbolic meaning were recognized instantly by all Muslims: Badr was the place outside Medina where Muhammad's forces scored their first significant military victory over the Quraish, an event that convinced them God was indeed on their side and one that stands as a landmark in Islamic history.

For all their ethnic and political diversity, Muslims the world over do share a common history and heritage within the faith that link them to each other even when their governments or their compatriots are at odds. Events such as Badr, part of their shared memory, are understood as religious events, manifestations of God's will, unlike, for example, the Spanish conquest of Mexico, which was an imperial, not a Christian, event. Differences over detail and tactics—to what extent Islamic law should be applied in the modern state, how best to help the Palestinians—divide governments and political groups, but individual Muslims from any group or society can meet anywhere in the world and find an instant bond in their common faith and heritage.

The greatest living symbol of the fraternity of Islam is the annual pilgrimage to Mecca. More than a million men and women make the journey each year. They are blacks and Berbers, Arabs and Indians, peasants and generals, Iranian Shiites and Iraqi Sunnites. In the act of pilgrimage they are all indistinguishable in their white raiment as they bow in prayer, all equals before God.

Muslims still pursue the ideal of fraternity that has eluded them since the eighth century. From time to time, in small ways, they achieve it. A good example has occurred during the war between Iran and Iraq, when Muslims in several nations put aside their differences over that conflict in the interest of religion. Recently a group of Muslim Arabs who are citizens of Israel were able to make the pilgrimage for the first time since the creation of the Jewish state because of the kind of supranational pan-Islamic cooperation that the Muslim ideal espouses. Buses chartered in Iran crossed into Turkey, avoiding Iraq, and thence into Syria and Jordan. Iranian buses were used because neither the Jordanians nor the Syrians wanted to be in the position of aiding Israelis, but both Jordan and Syria, though supporting different sides in the war, allowed the passage across their territory so fellow-Muslims could make the pilgrimage. The buses went to the Allenby Bridge, which links Jordan to the Israeli-occupied West Bank, picked up the pilgrims and took them to Mecca. The Saudis had given them permission to enter the country.

Jordan was supporting Iraq in its war with Iran. Turkey was a secular state, Iran a religious one. All of the countries involved have different policies toward Israel. But the ideal of the pilgrimage and the fraternity of Islam prevailed over other concerns.

Such incidents illustrate the durability and the appeal of the Islamic message. Muhammad taught that religion, not tribe or geography, should be the basis of human relationships. Shared history and shared experience create shared perceptions: an appeal for the restoration of the Islamic way of life and a purge of Western colonial influence carries the same connotations in Algeria as in Indonesia, though the differences in response may be as great as the differences between the two countries themselves.

The pilgrimage to Mecca is the greatest living symbol of the fraternity of Islam. Egypt's late President Sadat made the pilgrimage in 1971.

United Press International Photo

The shared ideal explains why Muslims cling to their faith and why it is vigorous and growing. In this century the Islamic world has been transformed from an impoverished appendage of European economic and military power to a self-confident and independent group of nations seeking their own political formulas. At the same time an explosion of material wealth, not just in the Arab oil states but in Nigeria and Indonesia as well, has transformed the physical environment in which Muslims live. In times of change and stress, the religion provides continuity, a moral and cultural pole by which the transformations are measured, judged and controlled.

Islam is a flexible faith. Lacking a central doctrinal authority, each individual and community can choose its own course within the faith. The struggle to decide what that course should be may cause friction and even bloodshed, as in Iran and Syria, but the framework, the context, will be the moral code and cultural heritage of Islam. The more vigorous the assault on Islamic tradition, the more vigorous the response of its defenders.

There is, however, no consistency and little predictability in the choices that Islamic societies make. All that can be said with confidence is that Islam will be the measuring stick by which those choices are judged.

A traveler going directly from the Libyan capital of Tripoli, for example, to Dubai on the Persian Gulf would hardly believe the two communities had any cultural, linguistic or political ties—except, of course, at the mosque. Tripoli, after more than a decade of Qaddafi's Islamic and Arab nationalist policies, is austere, almost spartan: public entertainment is scarce, alcohol and nightclubs are banned, all public signs and documents are in Arabic only, all banks are nationalized, and the city has been largely purged of foreign merchants and shopowners. Dubai is wide open. Alcohol is sold legally in stores and elegant restaurants, trendy boutiques with English and French names sell the latest European and American fashions and books, and commerce is dominated by Britons and Pakistanis. It is possible to spend several days at a time in Dubai without hearing Arabic spoken.

Neither of those extremes, however, necessarily represents the future course of Islamic societies. Most of the Muslim world is in a state of transformation and of political and social evolution. It is too soon to predict what kind of communities will emerge or whether the inconsistencies will be resolved.

These questions are of more than abstract interest to the United States and Europe. It is a truism of international affairs that the Muslim world is a turbulent and unpredictable place where Western interests have been jolted time and again in the past 15 years: war between the Arabs and Israel that closed the Suez Canal in 1967, and war again in 1973; war that split Pakistan and involved India in 1971; the Arab oil embargo of 1973-74 and the rise of the Organization of Petroleum Exporting Countries; the Iranian revolution; the Soviet invasion after coup and countercoup in Afghanistan; Libyan attacks on Chad and the Sudan; the civil war in Lebanon; the murder of Sadat.

## *Lessons of Recent History*

In trying to understand developments in the Muslim countries, it is important to remember that they are a diverse community in a time of rapid change and upheaval. In those conditions, the faith that all Muslims share is a strong force and an appealing rallying-point for political action. Recent events teach several lessons:

1. Islam is a vigorous, growing, and self-confident force. It is not going to go away or compromise itself in the interest of any "strategic consensus" designed in Washington. In the words of journalist Jansen, "Militant Islam is no mere fashion or passing fad. It has always been and for a long while to come will remain a permanent factor in the life of the Islamic world. Recent events in Iran and Pakistan in particular have merely enhanced the already-existing steady pressure of militant Islam to rise to the surface of national life in all Muslim countries and then to take control of that national life. Hence the rest of the non-Muslim world is, to use a current vulgarism, 'stuck with' militant Islam and will have to learn to live with it."

2. It cannot be assumed that technological progress and material change in Muslim countries will lead their people to share Western social ideas or world outlook. In the imperialist era, approximately 1800 to 1960, the way to prosperity and influence in much of the Muslim world lay in mimicry of the dominant European power: learning English or French or Italian, mastering European military techniques, adopting European forms of expression in art and literature, working out political questions in European terms of parliaments and constitutions and political parties. Now that the imperial era has ended, it is no

longer necessary for Muslim societies to shape themselves according to imported standards, and many of them will not do so, as events in Libya and Iran have shown.

Put crudely, the people of the Muslim world have no obligation whatsoever to adopt Western political or social values; in fact, they are often repelled by the materialism, violence and erosion of family life and discipline that they associate with Western culture. Many Muslims have learned that it is possible to achieve material progress, to build roads and computerized factories and petrochemical plants, without letting go of a way of life and a set of values that offer them the comforts of tradition and discipline.

3. Islam, as an all-embracing political, social, economic and intellectual system, is not inherently hostile to or incompatible with Western strategic and economic interests. Nothing in Islam forbids pragmatism and flexibility in a ruler. Events in Iran are not necessarily representative: the Iranians had a unique grudge against the United States because of the relationship between Washington and the shah's regime. In other Muslim countries, the United States and its ideals are often admired and respected, as was shown by the mass enthusiasm that greeted President Richard M. Nixon when he visited Egypt to restore relations in 1974, after years of hostility. It should be possible to maintain constructive working relationships with Muslim countries, provided the United States makes no attempt to tell them how to conduct their domestic affairs, and refrains from sitting in judgment on their way of life. U.S. support for Israel and opposition to the Arab position on Palestine are of course a constant irritant in relations with Muslim states. But only Iraq has terminated diplomatic relations because of it.

Anyone who has had any personal acquaintance with the Muslim world knows that the vast majority of Muslims are ordinary working folk—farmers, clerks, soldiers and factory hands—who go peacefully about their business. They are not scimitar-wielding vigilantes or hot-eyed radicals. Mobs can be manipulated, of course, as in the attack on the American embassy in Islamabad, Pakistan, in 1979, but that is true in non-Muslim countries as well. In general, Muslim countries, however fundamentalist or doctrinaire in their domestic policies, can be constructive partners if treated with respect.

4. The United States, as historian Kramer observes in his essay "Political Islam," "cannot successfully depict itself as a 'friend of Islam,' and should not try. The Germans, Italians, French, British and Russians each used this ploy at one time or another over the past century, with almost no success. There is nothing uniquely attractive about our society, our economic system or our form of government from some abstract Islamic perspective."

The corollary to this is that the old bromide about Muslim aversion to communism because it is atheistic has no relevance to contemporary international relations. On an individual basis, most Muslims would probably oppose any atheistic doctrine, but that has nothing to do with the foreign policy of Islamic nations. At one time or another, the Soviet Union has had close working relationships with several Muslim countries: Egypt, Somalia, Iraq, South Yemen, Libya, Syria. Even such conservative monarchist states as Jordan and Kuwait have friendly relations with Moscow; both have purchased Soviet weapons.

These decisions are made pragmatically, not on the basis of religion. To Qaddafi of Libya or Assad of Syria or PLO leader Yasir Arafat, it means little that the United States is a democratic country committed to freedom of religion while the Soviet Union is not; the Soviets provide weapons and machines and votes in the United Nations, while the United States supports Israel. If Iraq has suppressed its Communist party, it is because the Communists threatened Baathist power, rather than because they are atheists.

5. Pan-Islam is a chimera. There is not, and there is not likely to be, any Islamic political movement that crosses national boundaries and overrides local interests to forge a multinational force. Muslim governments often profess unity, but they do not achieve it. Even if a fundamentalist government were to come to power in, say, Tunisia, the similarity of religious outlook with that of Libya would not necessarily end the Tunisian-Libyan dispute over oil exploration rights in the Gulf of Gabès. Some interests cannot be subordinated to religion.

## Brothers All?

Muhammad taught that "all Muslims are brothers." The Islamic nations, at a summit conference in Taif, Saudi Arabia, in 1981, reaffirmed their belief that Muslims, "despite the differences in language, color, countries and situation, are one nation, holding on to the bond of Islam and inspired in their life by a course on which they do not differ, and they derive their ideological source from a common heritage of civilization and shoulder one mission in this world." But neither Iran nor Egypt was represented at that gathering because of differences with their fellow Muslims. And some of those who were represented—Syria and Iraq, Morocco and Algeria, Libya and the Sudan—are set against each other in bitter disputes that outlived the conference.

Iran's Khomeini said as he took power in 1979, "I hope that all Islamic nations, which have been set against one another and divided by the evil foreign propaganda against them, will wake up and join hands to form a great Islamic government under the banner of 'There is no God but Allah' and prove victorious the whole world over." Many Muslims share that aspiration. But it is naive or demagogic to say that Muslims have been set against each other by "evil foreign propaganda." The truth is that political unity has eluded Muslims since the reign of the Caliph Uthman, 14 centuries ago, and is likely to continue to do so.

Fazlur Rahman, a prominent Muslim scholar, says in *Islam* that gestures toward Islamic unity such as the establishment of a permanent "Islamic secretariat" at Jiddah are prompted by "the intense emotional attachment that an average Muslim feels toward Islam and Islamic unity. Generally speaking, however, for the ruling elites it is more a matter of nostalgia for the shared historic past, heightened by bitterness against Western hegemony, than a conscious vision of an Islamic sociopolitical order." There is, in fact, no generally accepted "vision of an Islamic sociopolitical order," and none is likely to emerge, given the divergence of strongly held views about what Islam requires of state and citizen.

Reports of an "Islamic resurgence" must be measured against

centuries of political reality. There is no Islamic resurgence if the term is taken to mean a collective effort by all Muslims to unite under the banner of Islam and march together, as they did in the seventh century. The term has meaning only as it describes a growing desire of individuals and groups to reassert and promote Islam as an alternative to materialism, petty politics, corruption, secularism and permissiveness.

In that sense, Islam is a strong, assertive force. It is probable that it will assert itself vigorously within a generation in more countries—Indonesia perhaps, or the Sudan, or Morocco. But from the point of view of American planners, that is not necessarily an unfavorable trend. Islam preaches justice, mercy, social stability, and generosity to the weak and afflicted. As a basis for domestic policy, those principles are unexceptionable; outsiders cannot and should not attempt to deter political movements based on them. In Kramer's words, "We cannot aspire to arrest change, and we appear unprepared to intervene with conviction in the affairs of independent Muslim nations." What we can do is offer friendship and cooperation without condescension. We can respect people whose outlook on life is different from our own. We can disabuse ourselves of the distorted notions about Islamic beliefs and practices that influence our judgment about Islamic politics. And we can set aside the fear of Islam that has led us down so many false paths in the past.

# Talking It Over

*A Note for Students and Discussion Groups*

This pamphlet, like its predecessors in the HEADLINE SERIES, is published for every serious reader, specialized or not, who takes an interest in the subject. Many of our readers will be in classrooms, seminars or community discussion groups. Particularly with them in mind, we present below some discussion questions—suggested as a starting point only—and references for further reading.

## Discussion Questions

What factors in recent years have contributed to the resurgence of Islamic fundamentalism and to the movement away from mimicry of European powers?

In light of recent developments in Iran and Egypt, how do you view the growing transnational appeal of Islamic fundamentalism?

How do the Christian and Muslim faiths differ with regard to religious involvement in matters of state?

In the Islamic state, is it possible successfully to separate religion and politics in the affairs of government?

What are the differing views on the proper role for the ayatollahs in Iranian politics?

Is religion the cause of the political instability that has characterized the recent history of the Islamic world? If not, what are the causes?

Is Islam compatible with Western objectives in international politics and economics?

## READING REFERENCES

Andrae, Tor, *Mohammed: The Man and His Faith.* New York, Harper & Row, 1977. A basic biography of the prophet.

Antonius, George, *The Arab Awakening.* New York, Putnam's, 1946. The classic study of the rise of Arab nationalism.

Esposito, John L., ed., *Islam and Development.* Syracuse, N.Y., Syracuse University Press, 1980. Essays on current trends in the Islamic world.

Farah, Caesar E., *Islam: Beliefs and Observances,* 3rd ed. Woodbury, N.Y., Barron's Educational Series, 1982. A basic introduction to the Muslim religion.

Hitti, Philip K., *Islam: A Way of Life.* Minneapolis, University of Minnesota Press, 1970. A study of Islamic history and culture.

Jansen, G.H., *Militant Islam.* New York, Harper & Row, 1980. An analysis of Islamic militancy in the contemporary world.

Kramer, Martin, "Political Islam." *Washington Papers* 73. Beverly Hills, Cal., Sage Publications for the Center for Strategic and International Studies (Georgetown University), 1980. A brief study of contemporary Muslim political affairs.

Lewis, Bernard, *The Arabs in History.* New York, Harper & Row, 1950. A standard work on the history and development of the Arab world.

Lippman, Thomas W., *Understanding Islam: An Introduction to the Moslem World.* New York, New American Library, 1982. An introductory study of the Muslim faith and Islamic history.

Rahman, Fazlur, *Islam,* 2nd ed. Chicago, University of Chicago Press, 1979. A scholarly analysis of the legal and philosophical development of Islam.

Tabataba'i, Allamah Sayyid Muhammad Husayn, *Shi'ite Islam.* Albany, N.Y., State University of New York Press, 1977. The history and basic beliefs of the Shiite branch of Islam by a prominent Iranian scholar.

---

*Cover photographs, left by Robert Azzi/from Woodfin Camp; upper right, Russell Munson © 1982. Reprinted with permission. With thanks to the Exxon photo library for its assistance.*

# THE PEOPLES OF ISLAM

| COUNTRY | TOTAL POPULATION | % OF MUSLIMS |
|---|---|---|
| Afghanistan | 14,702,000 | 99 |
| Albania | 2,626,000 | 70 |
| Algeria | 18,249,000 | 99 |
| Bahrain | 365,000 | 100 |
| Bangladesh | 88,092,000 | 83 |
| Benin | 3,379,000 | 12 |
| Brunei | 199,000 | 60 |
| Bulgaria | 8,892,000 | 13 |
| Burma | 31,800,000 | 4 |
| Burundi | 4,314,000 | 2 |
| Cameroon | 8,168,000 | 17 |
| Central African Republic | 2,418,000 | 8 |
| Chad | 4,523,000 | 50 |
| Comoros | 323,000 | 95 |
| Cyprus | 614,000 | 18 |
| Djibouti | 314,000 | 94 |
| Egypt | 40,958,000 | 94 |
| Ethiopia | 31,743,000 | 45 |
| Fiji | 621,000 | 8 |
| Gambia | 584,000 | 85 |
| Ghana | 11,741,000 | 12 |
| Greece | 9,100,000 | 2 |
| Guinea | 5,276,000 | 75 |
| Guinea-Bissau | 634,000 | 30 |
| Guyana | 824,000 | 9 |
| India | 669,785,000 | 11 |
| Indonesia | 148,085,000 | 90 |
| Iran | 37,582,000 | 98 |
| Iraq | 12,907,000 | 90 |
| Israel | 3,663,000 | 11 |
| Ivory Coast | 7,455,000 | 22 |
| Jordan | 3,055,000 | 92 |
| Kenya | 15,364,000 | 7 |
| Kuwait | 1,278,000 | 99 |
| Lebanon | 2,943,000 | 44 |
| Liberia | 1,789,000 | 15 |
| Libya | 2,873,000 | 97 |
| Madagascar | 8,358,000 | 7 |
| Malawi | 5,861,000 | 5 |
| Malaysia mainland | 11,068,000 | 53 |
| Sabah | 990,000 | 38 |
| Sarawak | 1,222,000 | 23 |
| Maldives | 144,000 | 100 |
| Mali | 6,350,000 | 90 |
| Mauritania | 1,558,000 | 100 |
| Mauritius | 933,000 | 16 |
| Mongolia | 1,639,000 | 4 |
| Morocco | 19,751,000 | 99 |
| Mozambique | 10,108,000 | 11 |
| Nepal | 14,028,000 | 5 |
| Niger | 5,133,000 | 80 |
| Nigeria | 74,604,000 | 47 |
| Oman | 565,000 | 100 |
| Pakistan | 80,171,000 | 97 |
| Peoples' Republic of China | 1,017,477,000 | 3 |
| Philippines | 46,893,000 | 4 |
| Qatar | 167,000 | 100 |
| Saudi Arabia | 8,103,000 | 100 |
| Senegal | 5,519,000 | 80 |
| Sierra Leone | 3,351,000 | 30 |
| Singapore | 2,361,000 | 15 |
| Somalia | 3,469,000 | 100 |
| South Africa | 28,094,000 | 20 |
| Sri Lanka | 14,502,000 | 6 |
| Sudan | 20,941,000 | 73 |
| Surinam | 98,000 | 20 |
| Syria | 8,395,000 | 88 |
| Tanzania | 17,358,000 | |
| mainland | | 30 |
| Zanzibar | | 98 |
| Thailand | 46,350,000 | 4 |
| Togo | 2,528,000 | 5 |
| Trinidad & Tobago | 1,136,000 | 6 |
| Tunisia | 6,412,000 | 95 |
| Turkey | 44,236,000 | 99 |
| Uganda | 13,225,000 | 10 |
| U.S.S.R. | 263,818,000 | 16 |
| United Arab Emirates | 862,000 | 96 |
| Upper Volta | 6,656,000 | 20 |
| Western Sahara Region | 75,000 | 100 |
| Yemen (Aden) | 1,781,000 | 100 |
| Yemen (Sana) | 5,125,000 | 100 |
| Yugoslavia | 22,174,000 | 12 |

Sources:
U.S. State Department Fact Book, 1979.
The Muslim Peoples, A World Ethnographic Survey, Richard W. Weekes, 1978.
U.S. State Department Country Offices.
The Embassy of Nepal.

*The above chart and map on page 6 were originally developed by the National Committee to Honor the Fourteenth Centennial of Islam. Copyright © 1980. Reprinted with permission.*

## *FORTHCOMING ISSUE*

### *The Third World: Exploring U.S. Interests*
*by John W. Sewell and John A. Mathieson*

*Despite increasing evidence of the developing countries' ability to influence Americans' security and standard of living, policy-makers in both the public and private sectors assign relations with the third world a low priority. U.S. strategic, political and economic interests in the third world and the need for a new strategy to meet those interests are explored in the next issue.*